A3 Problem Solving
for Healthcare

A3 Problem Solving for Healthcare

A Practical Method for Eliminating Waste

Cindy Jimmerson

Illustrations by Amy Jimmerson

+Healthcare Performance Press

A Division of Productivity Press

Most Healthcare Performance Press books are available at quantity dis-
counts when purchased in bulk. For more information contact our Customer
Service Department (888-319-5852). Address all other inquiries to:

Healthcare Performance Press, a division of Productivity Press
444 Park Avenue South, 7th Floor
New York, NY 10016
United States of America
Telephone: 212-686-5900
Fax: 212-686-5411
E-mail: info@productivitypress.com
HCPpress.com

Library of Congress Cataloging-in-Publication Data

Jimmerson, Cindy LeDuc.
    A3 problem solving for healthcare : a practical method
for eliminating waste / Cindy Jimmerson ; illustrations by
Amy Jimmerson.
        p. cm.
Includes bibliographical references and index.
ISBN 978-1-56327-358-2 (alk. paper)
    1. Health services administration.   2. Health facilities—
Business management.   3. Problem solving.   I. Title.

    [DNLM: 1. Organization and Administration.   2. Problem
Solving.   W 84.1 J61a   2007]

RA971.3.J56   2007
338.4'73621—dc22
                                                            2007013329

11   10   09   08   07   05   04   03   02   01

Contents

CONTENTS

Acknowledgments

The author and illustrator dedicate this book to Chuck and Norma LeDuc, our parents and grandparents, respectively, for the many problems they've solved for us in our lifetimes.

AUTHOR'S NOTE

This manuscript has offered me a unique parental experience: writing a book with my own daughter. She came to work with me several years ago as a convenience to us both and has grown into a priceless asset. As in her daily life, her work life has added richness, perspective, and humor to my world— A million thanks to my beloved Amy.

I also extend my deepest gratitude to the National Science Foundation for the initial support of our work.

ACKNOWLEDGMENT OF CONTRIBUTORS

No solid literary work is conveyed without the support of others, and while I can't recognize the hundreds of people that deserve my most heartfelt thanks, here's a hats-off to a few who have contributed text and experiences to this specific book:

- My business partners, Mike Brown and Charles Hagood, and all of the staff of our affiliate companies, Healthcare Performance Partners and Lean Healthcare West.
- Kevin Brodt and Bern Roy, Lean Innovations, and the staff and administrations of Eagle Ridge, Ridge Meadows and Surrey Hospitals, Vancouver, BC
- Vicki Baum, Indian Hills Community College, Ottumwa, Iowa
- Dilesh Patel, eVSM, Cincinnati, Ohio
- Staff, physicians, and administration, St. Vincent Hospital, Billings, Montana

- Staff, physicians, and administration, Community Medical Center, Missoula, Montana
- Staff, physicians, and administration, LDS Hospital, Salt Lake City, Utah
- Durward Sobek, faculty, Montana State University, School of Engineering, Bozeman, Montana
- Dan Armstrong and Russ Fry, Cartel, Inc., Bozeman, Montana
- Kristine Mednansky, Senior Acquistions Editor, Healthcare Performance Press

Introduction

WHAT IS AN A3?

Before launching into the business of A3 thinking and A3 problem solving, many will need to know: What's an A3 and why is it called that?

In a nutshell, the A3 document comprises a format for structured problem solving, created with a pencil on a piece of 11″ × 17″ paper. Outside the United States, this paper size is called "A3," thus the name. Although it may seem simple in design, the development of an A3 involves intense thought. This book discusses not only the features of the A3, but how to create them effectively and how to use the A3 document for solving *specific* problems. Essentially, the book demonstrates the potential of A3 problem solving in the productive transformation of your organization. In addition, the examples listed in Chapter 9 serve to inspire you to think of a million ways to apply this extremely useful process.

A3: LIGHT THE FIRE OF PROBLEM SOLVING!

Welcome to A3 problem solving! When I took my first baby steps on the lean journey that has consumed my last 7 years, I had no idea what a ride it would be! Within a few short weeks of observing and experimenting with tools borrowed from manufacturing, directly at the source—the Toyota Motor Company, I was amazed and delighted to discover the potential of adapting these concepts and simple tools to healthcare and eventually to other service industries. The sterling features of the Toyota Production System (TPS) and the story of Toyota's own sustained success appeared like a beacon. As a company, they demonstrate a level of quality, safety, satisfaction, and economy that we, as healthcare providers, would love to boast in our work. These last several years, I have been rewarded in recognizing in other healthcare leaders and frontline workers the ambition to follow that same *ideal* light.

The Toyota Motor Company and other industrial leaders who have followed the Toyota model have achieved leading-edge positions in business because of their accelerated rate and sustained duration of problem solving. Their pragmatic use of problem solving to achieve exemplary quality and waste reduction has driven these companies to become top innovators in their fields.

Of all the lean philosophies and practices that I've learned from manufacturers and students of Toyota who have been my mentors, by far the method that embodies the concepts and strategies at the core of Toyota's renown is A3 problem solving. It is much more than a tool, although it is commonly included in the "lean toolbox." As the method and document are understood and practiced, a new way to look at work and to *think* evolves, not just on the job, but in the activities of our daily lives.

At the heart of my motivation for writing this book lies the desire to see healthcare organizations grow away from the "command and control" management structure that has limited our potential and transition to "thinking organizations." Stopping to really look at processes, or the way we work, removes us from the rut of always doing them the same way. In the course of our busy and complex work, it's easy to let *the way we've always done things* sponge the efficacy from our jobs. And with that efficacy goes the fun, creativity (and sadly), the quality and profit of our work.

Learning and living the simple, but powerful, A3 process poses one easy but effective way to achieve the transition to *thinking organizations*.

I hope that by introducing this easy-to-learn, easy-to-teach way to look at everyday work system problems, A3s will soon light the fire of logical problem solving in your life.

A Brief History of the Toyota Motor Company

When discussing continuous improvement, it is impossible to overlook the contribution of the Toyota Motor Company. The company's work has led to the development of this book and scores of others about TPS/Lean and process improvement. Toyota generously shares its knowledge with the world, and the world listens. Why? While lagging behind U.S. manufacturers in production after WWII, Toyota grew to be not only the largest auto manufacturer in the world—but for 57 years, the most profitable. This has led many to study what is now called the Toyota Production System (TPS) to learn how the company achieved its current market position.

The Toyota we know today started as a department within the Toyoda Automatic Loom Works, Ltd. The root of the Toyota Production System began with Sakichi Toyoda, who constantly focused on the elimination of all waste, to efficiently produce the automatic looms. While in the loom business, Kiichiro Toyoda, son of Sakichi, visited the United States and Europe to learn about the manufacture of automobiles. When orders for looms slowed in the 1930s, the family decided to move into the automotive industry. In 1937, the Toyota Motor Company, Ltd. was formally established.[1]

In the early 1950s, Eiji Toyoda and Toyota's chief production engineer, Taiichi Ohno, began experimenting with systems that would ultimately support their strategy to mold the company into a full-range auto manufacturer. The two men faced

---

1. Womack, J., Jones, D., and D. Roos. *The Machine that Changed the World.* New York: Harper Perennial, 1991.

many challenges, however, not the least of which involved the lack of capital resources to invest in a mass production system. As a result of their work, the Toyota Production System was born. The company's early motto from the 1950s, "Good thinking, good products," continues to live through expanded adaptations in many industries in the world today.

In the mid 1940s, the Japanese met an American by the name of Dr. W. Edwards Deming.[2] He believed that if Japanese manufacturers would build the best quality products, customers would buy. Quality had to be built into every step of the production process, and he promoted the training and development of workers to accomplish that task. His teaching came in stark contrast to the mass producers of the time, who inspected quality at the end of the production line and experienced costly rework. They also expected workers to focus on specific, repetitive tasks only, without the opportunity to improve their work, which led to poor working conditions and a frustrated workforce.

The leaders of Toyota took Deming seriously and focused on building the highest quality vehicles on the market. Taiichi Ohno, the general manager of Toyota, in 1950 concurred that producing superior quality could be their market advantage, but they could only afford such high standards if they were relentless about reducing waste in their manufacturing processes. Thus the Toyota Production System was born.[3] In Japan today, the highest award for manufacturing excellence is still the Deming Prize. Toyota has created a culture where everyone is challenged to eliminate waste and defects, and the company supports all employees in improving work processes. The Toyota Production System has helped Toyota become the world leader in auto manufacturing. This success is worth following as its culture of striving toward perfect quality, while relentlessly eliminating waste, may apply to any industry.

---

2. Walton, M. *The Deming Management Method*. New York: Putnam Publishing Group, 1986.
3. Ohno, T. *Toyota Production System*. New York: Productivity Press, 1988.

Toyota enjoys some claims to fame enviable in any organization. The company's record for employee satisfaction and low turnover is exemplary and not by accident. Toyota reveres its employees, considering each of them a scientist, skilled in problem solving and discovery. Every one of them is expected to think. This expectation proves fundamental in the company's structure as a learning organization. Each worker uses A3 thinking in his or her daily work, and the concepts behind this problem-solving method build confidence at the front line and in the boardroom.

Toyota recognizes its workers as the greatest company asset and has the best history of avoiding layoffs in the automotive industry. Development of individual talent and thinking form the backbone of the company's quality and fiscal success.

In October 2004, Art Niimi,[4] the CEO of Toyota America, spoke at the national conference of the Association for Manufacturing Excellence in Cincinnati. During his speech, to a packed room of 1,200 attendees, Niimi's single slide, which illuminated the back wall of the triple ballroom, simply read: *THINK DEEPLY*. The title of his talk was "Respect for Man and Respect for Mankind." No mention in title, slides, or content of cutting cost, creaming the competition, laying off staff, or taking over the world of auto manufacturing. With dignified presence and elegant manner, Niimi spoke only in reference to respecting the people doing the work, as well as respect for mankind and the earth on which we rely. His message was powerful and crystal clear: *think deeply*. At the end of this moving presentation Niimi responded to several questions from the audience—one especially poignant: He was asked why, with the success that puts Toyota in the global media spotlight almost daily, he or someone from Toyota hasn't written a book telling people how to do what Toyota has done. After a palpable pause and silence, as everyone in the room awaited his answer, he said, "If I did, it would only be two pages." The response of those new

---

4. Art Niimi: "Respect for Man and Respect for Mankind." Keynote address, Association of Manufacturing Excellence Annual Conference. Cincinnati, OH: October 2004.

to TPS/Lean was quizzical; they didn't get it. Those wholly familiar with lean practices completely understood the message: Making it complicated loses the essence of *thinking deeply*.

This message creates a dilemma for those who have lived and grown up in the world of "command and control" management. This outdated business model does not encourage employees to think deeply, but rather to report problems up the ladder, so someone else can, eventually, devise a quick fix. It has been unrealistic (and unfair) for management and the senior leadership team to create fixes for problems in work from which they are far removed. It has been the expectation of frontline workers to make those changes happen despite their eye-rolling acknowledgment that the fix would likely fail. This model not only fails workers but their organizations, by not encouraging *deep thinking* to be practiced daily by everyone. The knowledge locked in our collective intelligence runs the risk of being lost.

But change never comes easy. Folks who have been clocking in for years won't suddenly start *thinking deeply* simply because they are told to do so. And the number of workers that need to adjust, quickly, is staggering. That's one of the reasons A3 thinking and the practice of problem solving in this systematic way proves successful. A3 thinking forms a template, as well as a necessary crutch, to help transform any industry into a *thinking industry*. It is necessary to actualize this practice every day, in every department, starting now. The next chapter looks at the concepts behind this practice and will begin to pave the way toward *thinking deeply*.

The Concepts Behind A3 Thinking

2

IDEAL AND THE 4 RULES IN USE

At the conclusion of research for his doctoral work in 1999, Harvard Ph.D. candidate Steven Spear, with Harvard Business School professor Kent Bowen, described the concepts of "Ideal[1]" and the "4 Rules in Use." In their landmark paper, *Decoding the DNA of the Toyota Production System*,[2] they concluded that these simple concepts and rules were the fundamental drivers of the Toyota culture of work. Simple in concept, the consistent practice of Ideal and the 4 Rules is applicable to any business model. Figure 2–1 provides a checklist, showing how Ideal may apply to the healthcare industry.

The company's relentless efforts toward an *ideal state* comprise perhaps the most powerful notion credited to Toyota's success. As defined by Bowen and Spear, an ideal state for Toyota, and clearly applicable to healthcare or any industry, would include the features included in Figure 2–1.

These goals appear lofty and perhaps may be recognized as unachievable 100 percent of the time. However, harboring the elements of Ideal as the destination toward which to strive creates a consistent measure for strategic moves in an organization, or in simple tasks of work. When considering changes of policy or practice, simply ask, "Will these proposed activities

---

1. The concept of Ideal is originally credited to Dr. Russell L. Ackoff, (1919–). Reflections on the Idealized Design Planning Process, *CQM Journal*, Lee, T., Woll, T. Spring 2003: Voume 11, Number 2.
2. Spear, S. and H.K. Bowen. "Decoding the DNA of the Toyota Production System." *Harvard Business Review*, 1999.

IDEAL

☑ Exactly what the patient needs, defect free

☑ One by one, customized to each individual patient

☑ On Demand, exactly as requested

☑ Immediate response to problems or changes

☑ No Waste

☑ Safe for patients, staff, and clinicians: physically, emotionally, & professionally

Figure 2–1. Ideal, as it applies to healthcare

move us closer to Ideal?" If the answer is a resounding "yes!" move forward with confidence. If the proposal can't measure up to movement toward Ideal, review the points for a clear indication of where the plan falls short. Adjusting the plan toward an Ideal outcome is straightforward with specific direction for redesign. This simple conceptual image can reduce wasted time and efforts and create confidence in workers.

Let's consider the points of Ideal one at a time.

Defect Free

Any essential service industry such as healthcare (or public transportation, law enforcement, primary education, etc.) would like to claim that its product or service is "defect free." Every consumer of services would love to feel confident that services received (and paid for) are indeed without defects. But as many people know from countless, painful experiences— from the airlines delivering luggage to the incorrect destinations to healthcare billing systems creating inaccurate bills—defect free isn't usually the norm in service industries.

The term *defect free* says much more than "right" or "wrong." It suggests a level of superiority beyond "good enough," produced without problems along the way to delivery.

Many examples of receiving a requested service within a service industry recount a complex and time-consuming journey, which perhaps involved correcting real or near errors along the way.

A product or service without defects, particularly in industries such as healthcare, will produce significantly improved outcomes over a defective service. The apparent results of better care, patient satisfaction, and the dramatic scores in worker satisfaction will all be measurable. The cost of producing defect-free care to patients can be quantified—not only in happy, returning customers—but also in the reduced cost of remediation of errors and redundant activities by the labor force.

No Waste

Together with near-perfect quality, the constant attention to eliminating waste from all aspects of production and service is the hallmark of the Toyota Production System. Waste, in its most basic definition, includes anything that doesn't add value for the customer/patient or to the process. Consequently, when observing work in healthcare, it should be with an eye to identify any activity that impairs or delays value to the patient/customer *and* to the worker providing the service.

Taiichi Ohno, the man credited with the development of the Toyota Production System, adapted W. Edwards Deming's philosophy of flawless quality to Japanese auto manufacturing (see Chapter 1) with the inclusion of a second requisite component. As Deming proposed, "If you produce the highest quality, the rest will come" (meaning customer satisfaction, worker satisfaction, and profitability). Ohno added, "We can only afford to create superior quality, if we are *relentless* about eliminating waste."

Ohno also identified the "7 Mudas" (seven sources of waste) in manufacturing. While many more sources prevail, unique to each industry, Taiichi Ohno's list adapts to healthcare and most industries with only minor modification. It is relatively simple to identify specific elements of waste in daily work once the concepts are reviewed and understood.

No worker, particularly in healthcare where the well-being and safety of another human comprises the core of the work, appreciates having his or her time wasted. Recognizing the sources of *muda* in daily work constitutes the first step in eliminating waste, and eliminating the waste constitutes the first step in recognizing the value in a worker's time well spent.

The 7 Mudas correlate closely to the 4 Rules in Use. A short summary with definitions of the 7 Mudas for Healthcare follows;[3] an expanded table with examples can be found in Appendix A of this book. (See page 138.)

Confusion

A casual observer in a hospital, anywhere in the world, would likely be alarmed if he or she focused only on the questions of clarification asked daily. In one study conducted by Anita Tucker and Steven Spear[4] nurses on a busy medical unit were observed to experience 8.4 work system failures per shift. In fact, within scores of hospitals, of all sizes and levels of sophistication, similar results may be found, with nurses spending as much as 65 percent of their time looking for things they can't find, clarifying things that are unclear, and doing redundant paper work.[5] While these activities are necessary to get the job done or meet regulatory requirements, these are activities that don't add value for the patient. The very hardworking and motivated healthcare staff recognize these routines as a colossal waste of time and a source of great frustration, and are the best source of ideas for purging that waste.

"What do I do with this requisition?" "What does this order mean?" "Does anyone know what I'm supposed to do with this?" "Where do we store the _____?" These and similar questions are asked thousands of times in the course of caring for

---

3. Jimmerson C. *reVIEW* Workbook. Bozeman, MT: Cartel Printing, 2003.
4. Tucker, A.L. and S.J. Spear, "Operational Failures and Interruptions in Hospital Nursing." *Health Resources Research*, 2006, 41.
5. Jimmerson, C, D. Weber, and D. Sobek, "Reducing Waste and Errors: Piloting Lean Principles at Intermountain Healthcare." *JCAHO Journal on Quality and Patient Safety*, 2005, 0502.

patients. See Figure 2–2. Imagine if the work was so intuitive that the answers were built in to the process and the time currently spent and frustration currently experienced could be eliminated. The reduction of this muda alone increases the potential to capture a great deal of worker capacity, decrease worker frustration, and reduce the opportunity for errors in patient care.

Patient safety has always stood at the forefront of a caregiver's mind. The medical errors reported in recent academic and media exposés have alarmed and infuriated the general population and devastated healthcare workers. The failure of processes to support healthcare workers to perform their work efficiently is often rooted in confusion.

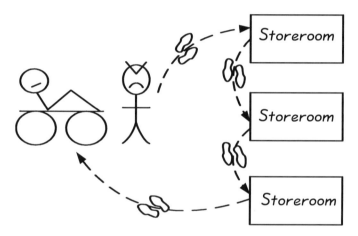

Figure 2–2. Unclear processes delay effective care and frustrate workers.

Motion

In many healthcare networks, necessary tools and supplies often lie out of reach, located in another department or building, and sometimes even on a different block or campus. *Motion* refers to the many physical steps required to gather the gear, confirm the orders, and organize the environment to care for the patient.

Redundant reaching for items that are not strategically placed, and walking to another location only to return to the starting point to resume work, exemplify motion that doesn't add value to the patient or customer. When observing and illustrating this motion, "loops" and "workarounds" in work become clear. Now imagine that the work could occur with continuous flow, in a straight line, without the loops (see Figure 2-3). Waste, created by ambiguous and redundant work, becomes easier to recognize and remediate when perceived through the 7 Mudas.

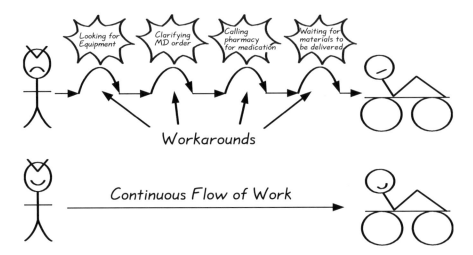

Figure 2-3. It's easy to see how "workarounds" delay care and decrease capacity of work.

Waiting

Delay in service often results from time spent doing nothing but waiting for something to occur, for example: waiting for a procedure to be completed, a medication to arrive, or a physician's order to be given.

Imagine the waste created when radiology staff wait for a patient to arrive from the ICU; the ICU and patient themselves wait for a transporter to arrive to wheel the patient to the radiology department—in the meantime, the transporter madly scrambles to find the right stretcher on which to transport the patient. Now imagine the discomfort, anxiety, and maybe even doubt that the patient suffers as he/she observes first hand this poor performance. Healthcare workers become accustomed to annoying lag time (consider the cost of the simple scenario above), however, the implications can prove clinically detrimental when a patient's treatment is held up. Every person who has sat in a hospital or doctor's office anxiously waiting for a diagnosis for him or herself or a loved one will attest to the risk, waste and distress created by delay.

Processing

Buried in the actual *work* of a broken process, or in the steps taken to accomplish a task, lies a tremendous potential for improvement. When unnecessary hands (and brains) touch the patient or product, waste ensues that can be avoided with a smart redesign. Clearly, one must never compromise the safety or quality to the patient when fixing any process, but rather enhance strengths and remove any weak sources of waste that don't add value.

Inventory

Obsolete, duplicated, or unnecessary stored materials prove, perhaps, one of the easiest sources of waste to identify upon initial observation. Inefficient storing patterns that don't support the worker's demands cause "supermarketing" or stockpiling excess supplies. With a goal that the workers have the *right item in the right place at the right time*, it's easy to observe a worker in motion and spot opportunities to put tools at hand. This source of waste is easy to measure because of its assigned dollar value. It's likewise easy to understand why a staff person hoards work items to avoid the workarounds involved with finding crucial gear when it's needed.

Patients awaiting services can also be considered inventory. Any interruption in flow that creates delays in care can be seen as an inventory issue. For example, having the *right patient at the right place at the right time* improves an unnecessary bottleneck and therefore adds value to each patient in the value stream.

Defects

Anyone who can read a magazine or newspaper understands the current focus on medical errors. *Defects*, as a source of waste in healthcare, prove staggering when one considers the measures of dollars, life, and work years lost, litigation, worker turnover, and general lack of confidence in healthcare as an industry. No professional organization or research team can measure the agony of loss or suffering caused by medical errors. In order to promote patient safety, the healthcare industry must strive to remove defects in work processes. While some errors are deemed "operator errors," behind almost every one of those is a process failure. From getting the right name in the database to administering the right medication, a process can be prescribed and followed that ensures patients are safeguarded within healthcare institutions.

Overproduction

Overproduction means performing more work than necessary to achieve Ideal. Redundant paperwork in healthcare creates a likely crisis in itself. Waste of patient time and the possibility of error when hastily answering duplicate questions continue as a common problem. That waste, compounded with increased worker time and potential errors from interpreting sometimes-conflicting records, ultimately decreases value. Automatic reports to consultants and automatic reporting of useless information to administration and regulatory agencies likewise eat time and dollars. Paperwork remains just one form of overproduction in healthcare. In many of our systems, workers do *too much* when *just enough* would meet the demand. When patient satisfaction is monitored, most want exactly what is needed to get them in and out of hospital services—no less, no more. Healthcare workers can combine compassion and care by removing needless activities from their everyday processes. In fact, avoidance of overproduction through unnecessary activities will greatly enhance patient care in the long run.

One by One

As our world community becomes more homogenous, sometimes the healthcare industry attempts to "globalize" service and assume that similar patients will require the same level and detail of care. On the contrary, the concept of each patient or customer as an individual must be kept at the forefront of delivering Ideal service. While mass production, whether of cars or flu shots, appears practical and cost effective, truly Ideal service must include attention to the requirements of each individual. Without the focus on each customer or patient when developing a flexible system, workarounds and rework, which complicate and delay the delivery of care, will inevitably occur. The added expense will defeat the purpose of "globalizing" the process in the initial effort. The point here is not to avoid standardizing work processes, but rather to implicate the importance of designing standardized processes that support flexibility in professional care, and enhance individual attention to specific needs. Processes developed without these features would cripple the caregiver from delivering truly Ideal care.

On Demand

In the last 20 years in America and around the world, the Internet has changed the way we shop—*on demand*. Think about it, a person can now boot up, key in an Internet address, search for a product, pay via credit card, and await the speedy delivery of his or her package from a distribution center that measures its accounts receivable in minutes, not weeks and months. The consumer acquires exactly what he or she ordered without leaving home, finding a parking place, or standing in line. As an industry that spends millions of dollars every year building, remodeling, and furnishing waiting rooms and parking garages, perhaps healthcare has something to learn from the fast-paced IT shopping market. It's time that the healthcare industry thinks outside of familiar boundaries and considers delivering Ideal service *right now*. Why can't someone have prescriptions delivered directly to his or her home, get cholesterol checked at a drive-through lab, or store personal medical records on a magnetic strip? Some of these concepts are already available and the future possibilities of on-demand healthcare are endless.

Giving customers exactly what they want, *when they want it*, forms one core principle of an ideal state. When observing work in progress and noting delays in care created by caregivers that wait for necessities from suppliers (e.g., the nurse waiting for a medication delivery from a pharmacy), it's evident that the patient suffers from the delay and the organization assumes the unnecessary cost.

Almost all industries, in an effort to create efficiencies, collect work in batches. When batching is unavoidable, the goal should involve sizing batches to create the best work delivered, as close to *on demand* as possible. When observing the work (always the first step in working toward *ideal*), looking for delays and other sources of waste in the batching process helps reduce batch size and move closer to the concept of delivering service "one by one."

Immediate Response to Problems

It is a clear responsibility of healthcare professionals to recognize when a process is not working for process improvement to succeed. Specifically defining what's expected of a system allows workers to easily recognize when defects crop up and trigger an immediate response to that failure.

Immediate response to problems identified by the people doing the work prevents the repetition of defective work. It also initiates the improvement that sets a thinking organization apart from "command and control management." Ideally, no defect or problem need transpire more than once and, in its correction, another layer of learning will have occurred.

How, exactly, does an institution achieve the Ideal state? (See Figure 2–4.) Bowen and Spear also interpreted four rules that Toyota follows to enable the company to create and maintain processes that move it closer and closer to Ideal. Significant and safe improvement can be made by assessing all processes and activities against these stringent measures.

The 4 Rules in Use

Rule 1: Activities (all activities of work in a process)
Clearly specified by:
- Content (what the work is)
- Sequence (in what order should it occur?)
- Timing (about how long should it take?)
- Outcome (what result is clearly expected?)

Rule 2: Connections
Direct communication between two people … (think of making a request)
- Direct (no middle man in the request)
- YES/NO answer (no "maybes"!)

Rule 3: Pathways
Steps in delivering the requested product or service
- Simple (involving as few steps and people as necessary)
- Direct

Rule 4: Improvement
- Direct response to problem
- As close to the problem as possible
- As an experiment
- By those doing the work
- Supported by a Coach

Source: Spear, S. and H.K. Bowen. "Decoding the DNA of the Toyota Production System." *Harvard Business Review*, 1999.

Figure 2–4. The 4 Rules in Use

THE FOUR RULES IN USE

Rule 1. Clearly specify all activities of work

Rule 1 states that the activities of work within a process should be clearly defined as to what should happen, in what order they should occur, and about how long the activities should take to complete. It also states that the outcome or goal of the work should be absolutely clear to the people doing the work.

In healthcare, violation of this rule frequently explains the confusion, errors, and general discomfort of healthcare workers. Perhaps because healthcare boasts a well-educated workforce, the unspoken expectation remains that each worker will decipher processes that support his or her work and that daily activities do not require overt definitions. This assumption frequently leads to several workers doing the same bit of work in different ways. This can add to misconceptions about what's been done and what should happen when patient care is transferred from one caregiver to another, when patients are discharged, and even when charges are created for services rendered! Specifying (or standardizing) the work is never intended to interfere with professional judgment. On the contrary, it should build confidence and reliability in processes that support effective work.

A clear example of this inconsistency is ordering laboratory studies for a patient in the emergency department. Any ED nurse, clerk, or physician may place the order differently than his/her peers if the steps in the process aren't clearly defined. Some may order through the computerized order entry or e-mail, some may call on the phone, some may pass a paper order through a delivery system or deliver it personally, and someone else may stop the lab technician in the course of work and make a verbal request.

The information on the request form may not be necessary for the test to be conducted or may be incomplete. The request may be delivered at the wrong time or to the wrong location or person. And expectations of the time in which the results of the test will be available may be completely unclear, which leads to unnecessary phone calls in search of the information.

The actual processing of the lab specimen may be flawed and inconsistent. If the test requires large batches, some technicians may process and report the results differently than others. Even details as seemingly meaningless as where the results are delivered, can create confusion and delay if the information doesn't reach the right person, on time, every time.

When using the A3 process to examine problems in processes, the evaluator asks the following questions of the worker(s) involved (and many more):

- Is it clear what should happen, in what order, and in what approximate time frame?

- Is every step in the current process adding value to the patient?

- Is the participation of every person who touches the process necessary?

- Does everyone who uses this process perform it the same way?

- How does a new worker learn this process?

- How did *you* learn this process?

- Approximately how long should the process take to complete?

- Is the expected outcome clearly understood?

Answers to these kinds of questions illuminate strengths and weaknesses of the process and contribute to ideas for redesigning the work.

Listen for the "negative keywords" that quickly become like fingernails on a blackboard—the ones that point clearly to an inconsistent and unreliable process. Here are a few of those words: *sometimes, maybe, if, it depends, possibly, perhaps,* and the classic answer to *"Why do we do it this way?"* which is, of course, *"Because we've always done it this way!"*

Rule 2. All steps in the request for a product or service are as simple and direct as possible (Connections)

This rule points to the complexity and variety of ways that a service or product can be requested or information passed from one person to another. The goal is that the request process be as simple (as few steps as possible) and direct (requestor gets as close to the person who provides the service or delivers the product) as possible.

Consider this familiar example to illustrate when Rule 2 is *not* happening: A customer calls a business' 1-800 number and gets a telephone menu; *if* the caller listens carefully and the choices are clear, he or she makes a selection on the phone, which brings this person one layer closer to the desired outcome. This can continue for 2, 3, 5, or even 8 or 9 times before this person acquires exactly what he or she wants—that is, if this person is listening closely and the choices are obvious. Should the caller become confused and push the wrong button, misunderstand the choices offered, or (horrors!) be disconnected, making a request could go on forever. See Figure 2–5.

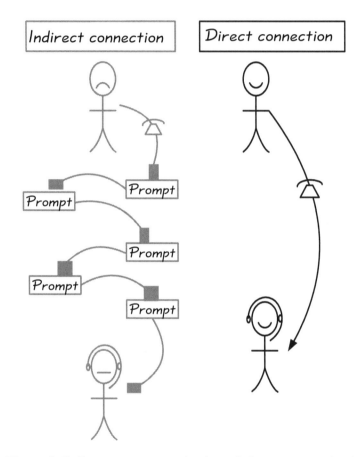

Figure 2–5. Consumers want simple and direct communication when requesting a product or service.

In 2004, Americans made close to 100 billion calls to 1-800 services. If the energy of that collective frustration could be harnessed (perhaps measured in the mm of mercury that our blood pressures rises.) the United States could likely eliminate its dependency on foreign oil. Ask people: "What do you really want here?" and they will resoundingly reply, "I want to talk to a human." It that somewhere along the line, the developers of telephone menus took their eyes off the customer and created a process that worked for them, not the consumer.

When beginning observations in healthcare, it quickly becomes apparent that processes, once assumed to be broken, involve service requests often as complex and unreliable as the steps of producing the requested product or service. The complexity of some request processes is staggering. When attempting to observe, evaluators must investigate the request process first—looking as far upstream, or as close to the requestor as possible—to identify the first snafu. If the request doesn't flow without interruptions, it will likely generate problems in the pathway of activities needed to produce the request. Correcting the problems furthest upstream can yield more improvement than may be assumed at first blush.

Reflecting back to the laboratory/ED example, observation of the way the service is requested can reveal some real surprises. In examining the steps in the request, the *number* of connections between people clearly signifies the complexity of the requesting process and identifies an opportunity to improve the process.

Ideally, all connections will be as direct as possible, with as few steps and people involved in relaying the request as is necessary to communicate the demand. Likewise, when the system works optimally, all users of the process will request it the same way. This makes the progress of the request transparent; that is, at any given time, the staff clearly understand how long it takes for the request to be filled and where the activity lies in the request process. The incidence of error related to missed or delayed requests will decrease by a factor of the number of eliminated options. And time wasted, calling to confirm receipt of requests and looking for results before the expected time, will be reduced. In essence, the system of requesting lab tests will be solid and the staff will have confidence that this system will work every time.

Rule 3: The pathway (or flow of steps) required to produce the request is simple and direct

The delivery of the requested product or service should involve as few steps and as few people as possible, always working toward Ideal, but never to jeopardize the quality to the customer.

From a high-level view of a system, the steps drawn on a value stream map clearly indicate this picture. In drawing the current condition on the A3, the movement of people and products and the loops in work that develop with the addition of people involved in a specific event, can be seen on a more specific scale.

Again using the aforementioned laboratory example, once the request has reached the laboratory, evaluators would look carefully at the steps and hands that the specimen passes through to completion, as well as the delays and sources of delay (traveling, in queues, unnecessary processing, etc.). This observation serves to identify opportunities to eliminate any wasted time or unnecessary activities required to produce the requested test results. Without this vision, *"good thinking, good products"* can't be a reality.

All of this information, gathered by observing, establishes the foundation for determining a better way to work, which follows the first 3 Rules in Use.

Rule 4: All problems are addressed as close in time and person as possible, under the guidance of a coach

This rule ensures that no error, once identified, will be allowed to reoccur. This rule recognizes the people doing the work as the most appropriate individuals to solve a problem. It also establishes the expectation that an experienced problem-solving coach, with time, designated outside the delivery of care, assists when a problem needs to be addressed.

A3 problem solving really comes into play in Rule 4. Ideally, the processes of work abide by Rules 1, 2, and 3 and are transparent enough to expose when one of those rules is violated. Rule 4 says now it's time to decipher *why* one of the first three has failed and rectify it, *as soon as possible after the event, involving the people doing the work*.

A3 Thinking Throughout the Organization

3

A3 problem solving uses a simple piece of paper and a pencil, but the impact of this problem-solving process proves much greater than the tool on which it is developed and reported. Although the paper guidelines, size, and self-prescribed limitations contribute to its effectiveness, the organization realizes much larger benefits as individuals engage in the method and begin to practice "A3 thinking."

Because A3 problem solving is logical, sequential, and clearly defined, the thought processes that support its success require minimal experience to introduce. Quickly, learners start asking questions such as: "What is the current condition?" "What problems are evident in the current condition?" and "Why do those problems occur?" and the big one, "Is the activity that we're examining essential to creating an Ideal system?" These questions initiate deep thinking instead of jumping to fixes which put a "Band-Aid®" on a complaint and may add more complexity to the system. It also steers the focus of the problem away from blaming workers or departments for a failure and searches directly for the root of the *process* problem.

A caution to any attempt at problem solving: It's easy in the zeal to fix things, to fall into the trap of fixing something that *shouldn't be happening at all*. Once A3 thinking becomes a norm, those traps will become more transparent and generate a step back to examine the bigger picture. This enables us to look at the whole system for opportunities to hone the processes that take us from request to delivery, defect free.

In itself, freedom from blame alters the way an organization looks at work and offers a breath of fresh air to the improvement environment.

A3 thinking becomes a practiced individual skill and proves equally effective in a group when addressing specific issues. (See Appendix H, for information on "conducting a lean meeting.") A3 thinking can permeate an individual's private life as well as affect activities at work, and it helps people improve relationships, as well as become better parents, coaches, and workmates.

So exactly what is A3 thinking? It's a structured pattern of thought that begins with identifying and articulating a problem that limits the system and prevents well-intended workers from delivering Ideal service. *It begins with never taking our eyes off the customer!*

The first step in improving a work process concerns this recognition of the problem, risk, or waste in daily work activities. A3 thinking involves deeply understanding the way work happens, based on direct observation, not assumptions. Repeatedly asking *why* it happens that way and putting that question to other workers affected by the process comprises the next step in achieving the insight that leads to the creation of a better way to work.

A3 thinking becomes the backbone of patient safety, with the continuous focus on the patient and his or her well-being.

A3 thinking means being constantly vigilant to identify waste in current work, which will result in opportunities to reduce and eliminate redundant activities.

Moving closer to *Ideal* is the uppermost and simplest objective to keep in mind. With every activity, the first question when looking at the current condition should be, "What about the way we are doing this work isn't Ideal?" And when we start asking "why?" roadblocks to *Ideal* occur, we can then discover which of the 4 Rules in Use is being violated. See Figure 3-1.

The 4 Rules in Use

Rule 1: Activities (all activities of work in a process)
Clearly specified by:
- Content (what the work is)
- Sequence (in what order should it occur?)
- Timing (about how long should it take?)
- Outcome (what result is clearly expected?)

Rule 2: Connections
Direct communication between two people ... (think of making a request)
- Direct (no middle man in the request)
- YES/NO answer (no "maybes"!)

Rule 3: Pathways
Steps in delivering the requested product or service
- Simple (involving as few steps and people as necessary)
- Direct

Rule 4: Improvement
- Direct response to problem
- As close to the problem as possible
- As an experiment
- By those doing the work
- Supported by a Coach

Source: Spear, S. and H.K. Bowen. "Decoding the DNA of the Toyota Production System." *Harvard Business Review*, 1999.

IDEAL

- ☑ Exactly what the patient needs, defect free
- ☑ One by one, customized to each individual patient
- ☑ On Demand, exactly as requested
- ☑ Immediate response to problems or changes
- ☑ No Waste
- ☑ Safe for patients, staff, and clinicians: physically, emotionally, & professionally

Figure 3–1. Adapted from the 4 Rules in Use identified by Bowen/Spear.

Rarely is fixing the first problem identified the only benefit that results from an A3. As the improvement team or an individual scrutinizes the process, this look under the microscope almost always reveals other related issues and opportunities.

Once people stop to *think deeply* about a problem, a bevy of issues will likely emerge.

This improvement work is always patient-centric, thus the issue under consideration is always stated through the eyes of the customer or patient. Identifying the customer is sometimes difficult. For example, if a doctor has to wait for an overdue laboratory report before he or she can make a diagnosis for a patient's admission from the emergency department to critical care, who is the customer? The patient is the true *customer* of the service, but the doctor is a *stakeholder* who is also affected by a low-value, high-waste process. The doctor may feel right-fully annoyed and concerned that his or her patient is not getting the prescribed care, and the doctor's time invested in finding the unreported information poses an obvious source of waste. The delay of transferring his or her patient out of the emergency department may withhold access to care from another patient awaiting an available bed. The critical care unit may be moving another patient out of the area and pulling in housekeeper resources to prepare for the patient, and on and on go the strings of attachment that make healthcare stakeholders so interdependent, each of which is affected by any fault in the process. However large the list of stakeholders, these individuals should not be confused with the customer. Repairing the process to better serve the true customer naturally results in added value for the stakeholders.

With the identification of the patient as the customer, improvement of the process becomes indisputable; after all, why do healthcare employees come to work every day, if not to serve patients? This approach enables everyone involved in problem solving to contribute toward improving the care-delivering process (or creating an accurate bill or delivering a hot meal) instead of focusing on blaming an individual or department for a failure. The focus on quality for the patient results not only in more reliable safety and service but also better relationships between individuals and departments—an important feature of A3 problem solving. Just getting the staff persons to look at the work through the eyes of their customers is profoundly effective.

TPS/Lean management does not mean managing by "project," although projects can be well managed using TPS/Lean. It's a philosophy of purpose—a consistent approach to providing Ideal service and providing a satisfying and safe environment of learning, experimentation, and reflection.

The simple but structured nature of A3 thinking and the A3 document make it easy to learn and apply quickly, in the course of work. The first successful improvement accomplished reinforces A3 thinking, and allows the alignment of new problems with the initial experience to visualize endless opportunities. As staff members share improvements with the easy-to-follow format, learning spreads to their peers.

A3s rarely fail when the process is followed, because of the depth of understanding achieved in the examination of the current condition and root cause analysis. Substantiated with validation for accuracy by the people doing the work, this deep understanding helps employees catch potential snags before reaching the "test" step. Many A3s require multiple iterations before successful completion, and almost always this results from an inadequate understanding of the current condition. However, each A3 will demonstrate *some* improvement and reveal even more opportunities. It is common to start an A3 with a goal in mind for changing a process and conclude, after several renditions, with a much different, but much richer, improvement.

Unlike customary problem reporting up the administrative ladder, A3 problem solving is done as close in time to the occurrence of an issue as possible, by the people closest to that specific event. This alleviates delays in problem resolution or solutions being contrived by administrators not close to the work. To be successful, frontline workers need enough familiarity and comfort with the process of A3 problem solving to feel confident initiating the process immediately. And there must be a structure of coaches to support the problem solver promptly. While that effort and commitment is not insignificant in the beginning of implementation, it pays off quickly with rapid dissipation of time-consuming problems. This method avoids the pitfall of problems being lost in the shuffle of multitudes of issues. And when dealing with and implementing specific issues on a local level, target conditions are tested before being introduced as house-wide implementations. The likelihood of innovations succeeding using A3 thinking results from the local nature of the process and wisdom of the problem-solvers.

MANAGEMENT CHALLENGES

One of the most difficult management shifts essential to the success of any lean implementation involves allowing (and expecting) work units to take the responsibility for redesigning their own work. The role of leadership changes from top-down decision delegation to coaching and approving process changes. Once engaged, leaders find that the A3 tool allows them to relinquish traditional power, because they too are confident that the method is sound and tested. Presentation of proposed changes (on an A3 document, of course) to the appropriate authority for each issue ensures oversight and engagement of the person in charge.

Persistent reverence for employees is a premium characteristic of the system created by the Toyota Motor Company. They recognize each employee as a scientist and the "resident expert" of the work that he or she performs. After all, who should know the systems of work better, both the good and bad features, than the people who do the work? And who better to redesign work than those who perform the work and have a clear mental image of Ideal for their own occupations?

Because A3 problem solving stems from the familiar *scientific method of problem solving*, which we all learned in our early education years, it's simple to follow the steps and arrive at a "scientific" conclusion, which holds many applications in a person's everyday life.

SPECIFICITY OF A3 PROBLEM SOLVING

Issues on an A3 are addressed in a scope that make it possible to address issues quickly and not in such a broad scope that it seems undoable. The size limitation of the A3 paper restricts the number of problems tackled within the problem analysis by the *5 Whys* and creates a "to do" list for the implementation plan. A person's eagerness to fix things, once and for all, instinctively leads him or her to assume diverse significant problems. Progress with an A3 comes much more rapidly and accurately when focusing on *specific*, significant problems (an idea Toyota has proved effective for 57 years). Although many problems appear small at first glance, their correction almost always bears greater value than first assumed. To quote another Toyota motto, "Take care of the small things, and the big things go away."

Another advantage to tackling specific problems is that selecting only the affected parties for issue resolution precludes the need for long meetings with multiple workers at great expense. Toyota conducts few large meetings; most work is completed by small focus groups, using A3 thinking and reporting with A3 documents.

ADAPTING TO CHANGE

While the A3 problem-solving method and document focus on identifying and correcting defects in a process, A3 is really about adapting to change. It may involve changing from a less effective way of working to a more improved method or changing from a previously accepted practice to a newer standard of care. Staff involved with the daily activities of work may identify the changes internally, or these changes may come as a result of an administrative change or a requirement of a regulatory agency. Whatever the source, the objective steps and simple, graphic design of A3 problem solving can clarify what's being requested by the change, why the change is necessary to get to the new target condition, and what is clearly expected of the participants orchestrating the change.

Because healthcare changes occur almost daily, in knowledge and process, this ability to create and communicate justifiable changes in practice, coupled with a consistent approach, strongly adds to the confidence of the staff affected by the change. Likewise, administrators responsible for the execution of a new policy or practice can understand and audit the change process by using the A3 document for reporting up and down the organizational ladder. Use of electronic conversions and data storing allows administration to monitor the progress of several projects simultaneously.

This consistent method of notifying and educating all staff of procedural or work-content changes builds on the use of value stream maps as tools for orienting new or experienced staff to a new area of work. If they learn a process illustrated with a value stream map, the A3 will effectively demonstrate any improvement made to that map and how it perfects the overall performance of the mapped process.

OBSERVATION

Direct observation of how the work currently occurs forms the keystone to success in A3 problem solving. To initiate a deep understanding of the activities of people and the flow of information, work observation occurs before the drawing begins. The observation includes engaging the people involved with the work to help identify roadblocks that prevent the work from happening with continuous flow. In healthcare, a current movement in quality improvement engages patients and families to ensure that the focus never leaves the patient.

The success of the observation depends on adequate preparation and inclusion of applicable workers, so that these employees are comfortable with the observation process and learn to recognize process problems down the road. Anytime staff members are included in observation activities, they need to understand that the minute-by-minute scrutiny is not about them as good or bad workers but rather analyzes the *systems that don't support them in doing their good work productively.* Staff will always view observation for A3 problem solving as positive and not punitive when they are engaged in the process and assured that the activity poses no personal threat. If the staff members are not accustomed to seeing upper management or other authority figures in the work area, watching their work in detail, it is even more important to establish comfort with observation activities (see box on page 32).

A3s should be a response to a problem at the front line, and therefore it's usually easy to elicit staff cooperation and get them to identify roadblocks, which regularly hinder the observed activity. Beware! Maintaining focus on the observed activity is important, for both the observer and those observed. It's easy to become overwhelmed with other issues that arise in the course of conducting the first observation.

In the course of a busy day, it is sometimes difficult to ask many questions of the worker while conducting an observation; maintaining a clear view of the action remains the goal. Finding a few minutes to validate findings with the worker (or workers) involved may require a return visit at a quieter time or an agreement to sit down over coffee to validate noted information. Workers love to see their frustrations substantiated, and this establishes enthusiastic cooperation for future improvement work.

A3 problem solving is easy to learn, easy to teach, and easy to coach. These features make achievement of improvements quick and increase motivation for future problem solving. It eliminates dependency on consultants and allows organizations to develop strong internal capacity to expand the culture of learning and improving. Coaching A3 problem solving develops leadership skills and strength and renews the bond of understanding between management and staff. Trust runs high in organizations with strong coaching structures.

Keys to engaging staff in observation early

Explain the observation objectives to the staff

- Engage the staff in pointing out roadblocks during the observation.

- Position yourself for good visibility but not an obstruction to the work.

- Use a personal watch for timing.

- Make notes to yourself that can be validated during a break in the work or after the observation activity.

- Don't interrupt the work.

- Validate the observation information with the staff after the activity.

- Follow up with the staff so they can see the results of the observation!

As a result, problem solving, as a process in its own right, becomes pragmatic and consistent. Workers soon rely on the method as a predictable and familiar way for the organization to approach improvement and orchestrate change. The often clichéd and undervalued terms "employee engagement," "owner-ship," and "empowerment" become realities as workers find their place in real and successful process improvement.

This confidence in *one consistent way to solve problems* is incredibly powerful. In an organization that practices A3 problem solving, when someone says, "Let's do an A3," everyone knows the steps involved and how employee roles will be engaged and affected. A3 problem solving provides coaches with a format to teach and support problem solvers and avoids creating a new process of issue resolution with each new circumstance that demands attention. Collaboration on improving processes that involve more than one department or organization occurs with a structure that uses common language and ground rules. A3 problem solving crosses those departmental borders smoothly. And each improvement is measurable in terms of real effects. Those measurements may be dollars, hours saved, quality points, and patient or worker satisfaction.

An intangible but predictable outcome of a process of problem solving in which different departments, administrators, and staff members have confidence is that animosity, "silo-ism," and blaming naturally dissolve as the focus points toward the indisputable purpose of improving the service (or product) for the customer.

The transparency of the improvement work becomes another natural consequence of using the A3 process consistently. With clearly specified and documented participation, it will be clear who is cooperating and being proactive. It is often possible to walk into a familiar work unit and identify the strongest staff member. Usually that person is an avid problem solver and one on whom other staff members can rely if conditions of work get complicated. By providing all staff with the same rules and tools, those less experienced and perhaps less skilled in problem solving will grow closer in skill to the ones at the top of the list as they practice and are coached using the A3 method.

Likewise, the process highlights staff members or administrators not contributing to the process and in turn creates just grounds for disciplinary counseling. Fairness and accountability replace blame and deceit.

The A3 Document

4

The A3 document forms the template and the record for problem solving. It is hand drawn on one side of an 11″ × 17″ (A3) piece of paper with a pencil. When its width is folded in half, it resembles two 8½″ × 11″ pages. Think of the left side as *the way things happen now* and the right side as *the better way to work*. Before you proceed, take a quick look at a finished A3 in Chapter 9 so that you can visualize the parts as you read forward from here.

VISUAL INTERPRETATION

The graphic nature of the A3 problem-solving document contributes to a quick and common understanding of the current condition. This visual way of "seeing" a set of circumstances that complicate work instead of "hearing" complaints, is refreshing and clear. Whether used in a group kaizen event to initiate resolution of a complex problem involving many departments and people, individually at one worker's desk, or in a formal report after the A3 is complete, A3 users unanimously favor seeing the current conditions and related storm clouds rather than hearing about them. Comparing the target condition drawing to the current condition diagram clearly demonstrates the suggested better way to work. Loops in work, workarounds, and rework become easy to see and eliminate. The question of moving closer to Ideal is simple to answer, when the activities and movement of the process can be read in graphics.

In addition to the features stated above, the reliability of common interpretation among members of the improvement team increases with illustration. People often become distracted when listening and focusing verbally. Visual interpretation is much narrower in scope than verbal interpretation. Visual messages leave less room for misunderstandings than the spoken word. Also, because the graphic is tangible and written in pencil, it can be revisited, revised, and redrawn, with all members of the team participating, until they agree on the end result.

The A3 document becomes the communication tool between the person observing and drawing the problem and the workers who will validate that observation. The steps are specific and if every step is completed, improvement in the work is inevitable. Caution! The only A3s that fail are the ones that aren't completed. The A3 is a process in itself and can't be considered complete until every step is exercised and documented.

The following sections look at those steps and review the thinking behind them.

THE ISSUE

Stating the *issue* of a new A3 may seem obvious, but there are some simple points to consider. The first, and often most difficult, is to focus on a *specific event or problem*.

For example, if a patient (Ms. Adams) was admitted during the night, and a prescribed medication to be administered at 9 a.m. hadn't arrived from the pharmacy at the indicated time, the tendency may be to focus on fixing the common general (and complex and large) issue, "missing medications." This would create an almost impossible, unfocused, and frustrating situation—a problem too large and diverse to get one's arms around. However, by focusing on the specific process problems that denied Adams her medication on time, a specific set of circumstances, which likely happens regularly because of a defective process, can be addressed. By correcting the process as it failed Adams, the fix will likely apply to all patients admitted during the night who need medications in the early morning. The acquired learning from the adjustment of a process for one patient can be easily transferred to similar situations.

Stating the issue through the eyes of the customer or patient is the second consideration. As discussed in the previous chapter, this seems obvious, but it remains much more natural to state the problem from one's own viewpoint: "I had to spend all morning finding meds that didn't arrive on time" or to blame another person or department, "The pharmacy never gets the new prescriptions filled on time." Neither of these statements puts the patient at the center of the resolution efforts and can generate feelings of hopelessness and ill will between departments.

Patient-centric statements of the specific issue make the work of improvement indisputable. This practice also assigns responsibility for improving the process to every person involved along the way, from request to delivery. Establishing buy-in from the staff to support any change becomes easier when the object of work (the patient) lies at the core of the improvement. Keeping the statement short (the document only gives you a limited space) forces the problem solver to focus succinctly.

BACKGROUND/MEASUREMENT

After defining the specific issue through the eyes of the customer, some background information may be needed to explain a situation that won't be apparent in the current condition drawing (e.g., if a department recently changed physical location, this might serve as useful background material).Within this box, some baseline data or circumstances that indicate the importance of this issue to the customer or organization should be indicated. Establishing a baseline to later measure against improvement is essential for justifying expense or activity to create the change. This can involve a measure of time, dollars, work units accomplished, or indicators of safety or quality. It's also important to indicate the significance of the occurrence. This section becomes important to the authority person, who will approve the upcoming implementation plan, particularly if money, risk, or manpower are required to complete the suggested countermeasures. The measurement can be recorded as text or graphs to illustrate significance.

In addition to the focus on the customer, one clever hospital uses an "F" (Frustrations) Scale as a standard for measuring how troublesome the people doing the work find the current condition. It's based on the commonly used 10-point pain scale that helps the patient describe the intensity or severity of discomfort, with "0" being painless and "10" being the maximum discomfort. In addition to initially recognizing the pain of the worker, the use of this F Scale has proven effective in building consensus for the importance of an improvement. It has also made it easier for staff to see value in the improvement if the problem is only partially corrected on the first effort. If the F Scale measure is reduced from 8 to 4, staff sees that the first improvement will make work more pleasing, even while waiting for another improvement phase to occur.

CURRENT CONDITION

The *current condition* is a simple sketch of the observed way that the issue occurred. It's done with a pencil, in the space provided on the left side of the preprinted A3 form. The simple line-and-stickman drawing should reflect direct observation of similar work occurring or a re-creation of the recent event and the people actually at the scene.

The value of drawing can't be overstated; being able to see the movement of people and information provides powerful information toward communicating accurate impressions of the work. The action of the pencil-in-hand on paper seems to educe the real message without words, using simple line drawings, stick-people, and arrows. The use of color to separate people from product movement and information flow makes a drawing easy to follow and tells the story that created the issue. The current condition is drawn after direct observation or interview of involved employees and therefore is likely fresh and as close to accurate as possible. Using a pencil to make the initial drawings on paper (or multiple colored pens on a whiteboard if doing the drawing in a group) generates a sense of involvement of all affected parties as they add their comments, corrections, and additions to the sketch.

The pencil's eraser also contains significant power. Using a pencil for the drawing states that the image is not necessarily final. It welcomes immediate input from affected parties. Willingness of the author to change his or her position on paper *right now* signifies the strong cooperation and endless possibilities of the process. Since everyone knows how to use a pencil, no one needs to learn a complex computer program or purchase inconvenient equipment. Pencils can go anywhere, so the drawings can be performed in real time in real locations for accuracy. The author can concentrate on the problem instead of being distracted by how to run the computer.

Mechanical pencils with replaceable erasers make great employee gifts, and a supply of good pencils should become standard equipment with the A3-sized paper.

With dynamic processes, companies can make great progress once they start to look at the flow of work activities. One reason that the concept of *continuous flow* proves effective is that it captures how the work occurs now (how the information and the workers, and oftentimes the patient, are moving), clearly indicating any disruption in continuous flow. The improvement team then progresses, asking *why* these disruptions in flow occur, identifying the root cause or the source of the disruption. The next logical event in the sequence looks at the work without the disruption and deciphers how to bring that reality to fruition.

While the concept sounds simple and logical, without this type of structure employees seldom stop and work through these easy steps. They tend, by nature or experience, to speculate on the source of problems and jump to a fix or blame coworkers, instead of ferreting out the source before devising a better way to work.

When observing and drawing the work, the movement of *workers, patients or products*, and *information becomes transparent*. All of these movements represent possible contributors to the unnecessary complexities of a system.

Information flow may seem like a small part of the health-care spectrum, but in the research conducted[1] in one mid-sized community hospital, workers spent at least 60 percent of their time looking for things they couldn't find, clarifying things that were unclear, and looking for information that was unavailable or wrong. With the escalating reliance on technology for communication, the complexities that interfere with continuous flow of information become more frequent and significant. The conundrum created by technology that doesn't support the work is a new millennium dilemma.

The fact that Toyota maintains an exceptional record of introducing new technology stems from deliberate and consistent planning. Before purchasing new IT, the company initiates A3 thinking and asks: *"How do we use our current technology now?"* (current condition) *"What about it is problematic?"* (storm clouds, see Figure 4–1), and *"Why do the problems occur?"* (root cause analysis). From there, Toyota may involve the vendors or developers and clearly show them the current problems, indicating how they would like the IT to work (target condition). Then the company realistically expects delivery of the product it needs. The A3 process and the graphic features of the A3 make requests of any vendor/supplier easier to clarify than a standard written or verbal request.

Figure 4–1. Each storm cloud represents a problem within the current condition.

---

1. Sobek, D. and C. Jimmerson, "Applying the Principles of the Toyota Production System to Healthcare." NSF Grant, 2001–2004.

Validating the current condition with staff, and getting staff input on paper so that it can be visualized, are two of the most effective activities of A3 problem solving. Only with this deep knowledge and agreement can a thorough understanding of how the work currently happens be achieved. As opposed to workers continuing to think of a problem or process in isolation, the group agreement assures accuracy, clarity, and buy-in for improvement. It's this enlightenment from the left side that makes the right side of the A3 so natural.

Once the current condition is deemed accurate by the people doing the work, problems with the way the work currently happens are identified as storm clouds, which are drawn onto the current condition sketch as close to where they occur in the work as possible. The following elementary questions should be asked with each A3 to initiate problem identification:

1. What about this current condition isn't Ideal? See Figure 4–2.

IDEAL

☑ Exactly what the patient needs, defect free

☑ One by one, customized to each individual patient

☑ On Demand, exactly as requested

☑ Immediate response to problems or changes

☑ No Waste

☑ Safe for patients, staff, and clinicians: physically, emotionally, & professionally

---

Figure 4-2. Ideal, as it applies to healthcare

2. Does work happen in a straight line with continuous flow? See Figure 4–3.

Figure 4–3. Continuous flow means work that proceeds without interruption or waste.

3. What roadblocks can you see that must be "worked around?" See Figure 4-4.

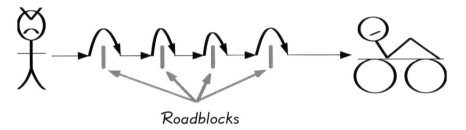

Roadblocks

Figure 4–4. Roadblocks deter caregivers from effectively serving the consumer/patient.

PROBLEM ANALYSIS

A recent favorable trend in quality and process improvement efforts seeks to determine the root cause of problems and stop the issue at its source. This grand move greatly differs from the practice of putting a Band-Aid® on a broken process. But finding the root of the problem may be confusing without some structure. Toyota's method of asking why five times (5 Whys), to get to the bottom of a problem, has proven both easy and enlightening. This problem analysis in A3 problem solving offers one more pragmatic step toward facilitating *deep thinking* about conditions that created the specific situations. Five whys is a concept; sometimes only three questions can transport an individual to the root cause and sometimes the list is longer.

Identifying the storm clouds in the current condition provides a base from which to start the 5 Whys. Each storm cloud represents a problem within the current condition and asking *why* the first time gives the initial peek into the root cause. The following outline delves into the reasons that a storm cloud occurs. Each subsequent *why* offers a deeper look into the answer to the previous why.

Incorrect charges to patients

why? The charges of another patient with a similar name may be captured incorrectly

   why? Confusion when more than one name is used for the patient (i.e., nicknames)

      why? Patient is not admitted with his/her registered Medicare name

         why? Admissions doesn't always ask for the patient's insurance card

            why? Admission activity is not clearly specified

Sometimes more than one element of information answers one question of *why* or adds information to the root cause. These statements are stacked, as in the example above, to indicate their reference.

Don't get hung up on counting the *whys*; remember that the point is to drill into the problem in order to understand it deeply and arrive at a root cause that becomes the detailed focus of improvement. While this appears, at first glance, as a lot of *thinking* for something that is likely a common problem, the payback comes on the other side of the A3, with the development of countermeasures to make things better. Once the root cause has been identified, the required fundamental changes become clear.

As the implementation on the right side of the A3 is developed, A3 authors can look back at the final *whys* and determine what specific activities are necessary to remove those root causes.

It then becomes easy to move forward to a target condition with confidence.

TARGET CONDITION

The *target condition* is the proposed better way to work. Like the current condition, it is represented graphically. This similar sketch, containing ideas for improvement, contrasts against the current condition. With two visuals on one piece of paper, it's easy to identify loops in work on the left side that are now absent on the right. Identifying the possibilities for continuous flow then becomes more evident. The comparison itself highlights the complexity in the current condition and pinpoints whether or not the improvement brings the work closer to Ideal.

Remember, this is an activity of improvement, not perfection. If Ideal is achieved on the first go, great! But if practical limitations allow only an incremental move toward Ideal, the effort is likely worthwhile.

As storm clouds were once placed on the sketch of the current condition to indicate problems, fluffy clouds, or positive and productive features of this proposal, may now be added to the target condition drawing. Like the storm clouds, they should be placed near the activity to which they pertain, and are best done in a contrasting color or line to not be confused with the work itself. Because this book is published in black and white, the following drawings are are not in color, but vivid color, used judiciously, can make an articulate statement. See Figure 4–5.

Figure 4–5. Fluffy clouds represent the positive and productive features of a proposal.

It's important in the target condition to indicate the anticipated measurable improvement. This is a reasonable and fairly accurate speculation because of the degree of understanding achieved on the left side of the page. This information can be compared with the initial measurement that was submitted in the background/measurement section of the current condition.

Just as in the current condition drawing, one author draws the target condition but includes ideas for improvement contributed by other workers involved with the process. As with the left side of the document, validation of the target condition is essential to foresee any complications that a single author may overlook. This collective validation strongly develops support and enthusiasm for making a change in old habits.

When projecting the anticipated measurement on the target condition, it must reflect the style of the statement in the background/measurement section on the left side of the page. For instance, if you use graphs on the left side, use graphs on the right side of the A3.

COUNTERMEASURES

The *thinking* that has gone into the A3 by this point is significant. The current condition has been observed, the storm clouds have been recognized and analyzed, and a thoughtful plan for a better way to work has been devised.

Developing *countermeasures*, or changes that must be implemented in the process to move from the current to the target condition is next. These measures counter the storm clouds, so for each storm cloud and its root, the question of what needs to be done to actualize the better picture requires definition. Without the structure of the activities on the left side of the A3, any countermeasure, though based on experience, would provide mere speculation. Warning! Many fall into this familiar trap by habit, as it may have been the expected way to work for many years. With patience and an adherence to the A3 method of thinking, however, old ways of working naturally fade into obsolescence. A3 problem solving uses reliable information and sound recommendations. They contain the built-in cushion of knowledge that the plan will be tested before implementation. Countermeasures are generally simple, strong statements like, "Notify patients the day before test time" or "install key-pad on pharmacy door." These statements don't specify *who* will make it happen, just *what* needs to be done.

IMPLEMENTATION PLAN

Most people understand the need to create countermeasures, especially when faced with the frailties of a system. During customary meetings, everyone contributes his or her best-laid plans regarding what improvements can be made. Unfortunately, once these same people leave their meetings and face a myriad of other demands, oftentimes those intentions get lost or delayed. The implementation plan on an A3 document establishes in writing *what* needs to happen, *by whom* it will be done, *when* it will be completed, and spells out clearly the expected *outcome*.

IMPLEMENTATION PLAN

What	Who	When	Outcome

This simple organizational tool sets accountability for the real tasks that need to occur in order for countermeasures to happen. If the countermeasures are *what* need to change, the implementation plan provides a roadmap for *how* and *when* this will be accomplished. The plan gives structure to the improvement work and gauges the necessary dollars, time, and effort required to make the advocated improvement.

COST AND COST BENEFIT/WASTE RECOGNITION

COST AND COST BENEFIT/WASTE RECOGNITION

Cost	$ $ $
Cost Benefit	$ $ $

When an A3 is presented to an administrator, his or her eye may wander to this box magnetically. As previously stated, this information would be questionable, without measurements that compare the current way the work is done to the anticipated improvement.

The *cost* space on the document refers to the cost of the implementation plan. How much is it going to cost, in dollars, hours, and so forth, to make the proposed changes? Because the plan has been sculpted with precision and based on real knowledge, estimates of the cost should prove fairly accurate.

Calculating *cost benefit* provides fair justification for the cost of the plan. Again, the savings or waste reduction may not be a monetary measure. It may be reflected in patient safety factors, quality of care, patient satisfaction, or workplace appreciation.

Outside of recording the return on investment for fiscal evaluation, one of the advantages of documenting the cost benefit is the valuation of worker time wasted. Staff members gain a real sense of the "business" of their work when they can see their valuable time being wasted in the current condition, the reduction of that waste in the target condition, and then a *real dollar* value put on that savings. Since this raises personal esteem and a motivation to be an active part of the improvement, it also reinforces adherence to the change.

THE TEST

As mentioned previously, A3 Problem Solving stems from the scientific method. No scientist would proceed toward implementation without a safe and measurable test or experiment to determine the effectiveness of the plan. The test results provide an opportunity for reassessments and adjustments.

As with the implementation plan, someone should be designated to conduct the test by a specific report date. The test may be conducted in the course of real work that is closely monitored or in a simulation environment. For example, if the A3 process has been used to design a change in registering patients in a busy physician's office, the test may be to perform the new process with one of the physician's patients for one day. That allows a limited sample of the new work to be evaluated in a short period of time. The team can look over the results and make adjustments, if necessary, before rolling the new process out to the whole clinic. Tests can be progressive; in the example above, the staff may want to add the patients of each additional physician in the office one at a time to continue monitoring and tweaking the system.

FOLLOW-UP

Once tested and implemented, close and long-term *follow-up* of the improvements made in a process need to be recorded. Again, the A3 document creates written accountability in the follow-up box, which includes, *who* will check the process, *what* measure or test will be used, and *when* the follow-up will be conducted. Depending on the activities, a recurring review of the implementation plan in progress may be needed. In the A3 examples in this book you can see that the follow-up box is bolded as a reminder for reviewing A3s. It is very important that this step is completed!

When developing criteria for follow-up, objective questions with yes/no answers or units to measure provide easy-to-evaluate and concise information. For example, perhaps in the scenario above, the issue was delay of patient care because patients arrived at the clinic without their essential insurance information. If one of the countermeasures addressed patients arriving without their insurance cards, it would be easy to monitor for a day the number of patients registered who didn't have their insurance card, both in the current condition and after the new process was in place.

The information gathered in the follow-up evaluation becomes the *new current condition* of that work. When conducting the analysis during this step, the same invaluable question is asked: Is this work Ideal? If the answer is no, and the review of the work reveals an opportunity to improve it, great! It's easy to continue to improve the process by moving that follow-up information to a new A3 form and starting the process again—

this time with a razor sharp understanding of the work, which allows the improvement team to hone the work ever closer toward Ideal. This practice further exemplifies A3 as a true method for continuous quality improvement.

Ultimately, the goal of improving processes is to make them so transparent that each and every worker clearly knows when a process is working smoothly so that they can immediately identify when Ideal *doesn't* happen. And the A3 process starts again.

How the A3 Fits with Value Stream Maps

5

Many manufacturing and service industry leaders recognize *value stream maps* (VSM) as the mainstay tool of lean management. This high-level analysis of the flow, from request to satisfaction of the request, shapes the foundation of subsequent improvements.

The visual nature of the VSM makes the view of the steps of work objective and states frankly, *how the work really happens now*. It also makes seeing where the existing problems and eventual opportunities lie. As opposed to talking about problems—wherein lies the potential for misinterpretation—the simple, pencil-drawn map leads quickly to visual identification of problem areas. Waste in the system is easy to identify.

Value stream maps differ from familiar flow charts because they illustrate what really occurs, not what people think should occur. Value stream maps also highlight the time between the steps when *nothing* is happening to move the product or process toward completion. This void is recognized as frank waste and can provide the first opportunity to shorten the total time in the value stream.

It is at this point, when the VSM has been used to its greatest potential to identify areas of improvement, that the A3 problem-solving method fits so well in the improvement scheme.

Value stream maps may be perceived as a tool that allows a person to visualize machinations of a process from 10,000 feet, and A3 as the view through a microscope. With a VSM, problematic areas may be identified, activities within the process boxes observed more closely, and *specific* problems recognized, that contribute to a less-than-perfect process. Many A3s may be performed on a problem area identified within the VSM. Each of those will contribute to improving the value stream, which can be seen when repeating the VSM after those improvements are made.

After identifying opportunities in the initial current state map, a *future state map* is drawn to establish on paper a better image of how the process needs to flow. This creates a clear goal for all members of the work team. A3s are the working improvements that move processes from the current state to the future state.

The VSM can be used in many ways. In addition to understanding the work for the benefit of improvement, once the future state map has been developed and improvements initiated, the map can communicate a clear vision to everyone involved of how the work should be done with the required changes. Ideally, an effective future state map lists all the activities of work in each process box in order and follows Rule 1, the result clearly specifying how each step of the process should proceed.

Imagine the applications for orienting new staff to a unit or existing staff to a change in a process! The visual progression through the activities of discovery and deployment make new processes easy to grasp, and *understanding a new way to work* replaces *training a new behavior*. The retention of material viewed on VSMs and A3s is much greater than with conventional training.

Many problem-solving processes begin with planning a vision of the future state. Without the deep understanding, built on direct observation of the work, the possibility of embarking on improvement goals that rely on opinion or past experience still remains. As we methodically follow the A3 process, it keeps everyone honest and current, as direct observation captures the reality of how the work is happening *now*. The constantly changing environment of healthcare and all service work requires that improvements occur with an accurate, *observed* knowledge of the current work. Figure 5–1 provides an illustration that visualizes how VSMs and A3s fit together.

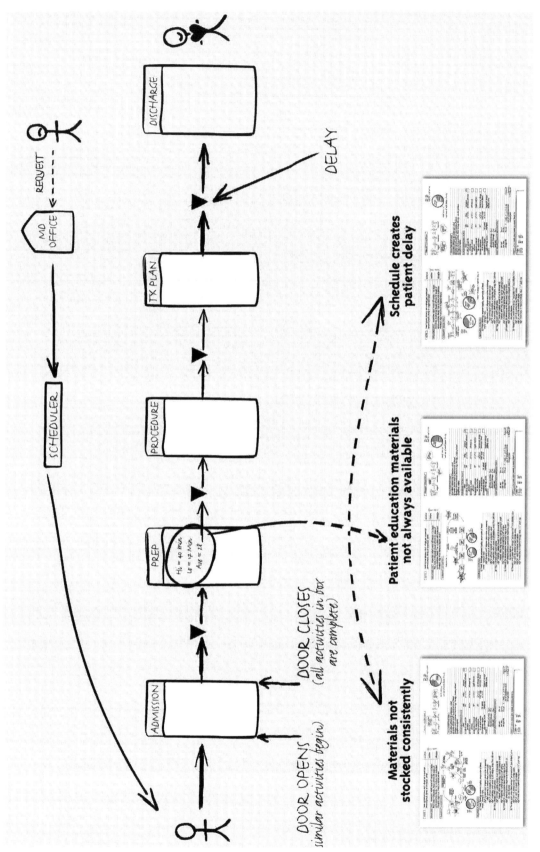

Figure 5–1. A3 and VSM complement the problem-solving process.

Many Other Uses of A3 Problem Solving and A3 Thinking

In addition to problem solving for specific process failures, many other opportunities exist in the activities of daily work to use A3 thinking. This chapter contains a short list of applications that have generated improvements in patient safety, as well as customer and worker satisfaction. The reduction in wasted time in meetings alone contributes significantly to the capacity needed to meet the growing healthcare demand.

LEANER MEETINGS

Many hard working managers and staff fall victim to the seemingly endless healthcare meetings. Using the same elementary principle of observing how the work currently happens, meetings can be evaluated for value using a tool like the one on the following page. (A reproducible copy of this tool can be found in the appendix of this book on page 148.)

This form allows employees to really consider the contribution of time, talent, and cost of meetings. It also offers the opportunity to reflect on the meeting material and really evaluate whether or not meeting time is used to its best potential. As with all A3 problem solving, this information can be the springboard for redesigning meetings to greater effectiveness.

Conducting lean meetings using the A3 process is a refreshing way to tackle the work of meetings. Consider the folllowing format (also available for reproduction in the appendices, page 149).

MEETING EVALUATION FORM

Name/Purpose of Meeting: <u>Plan a Party</u>

Time planned for meeting _____ Actual time in meeting _____

Participants: Clerical _____ RN _____ Manager _____ TechnicianMD _____

Administrator _____ Other _____

Number of minutes relevant to me/my work: (Tic marks ➔) _____

(From the current agenda, could you create an ACTIVITY DESIGN?

Activity   **Time * * 15 * * 30 * * 45 * * 60 * * 75 * * 90 * * 105 * * 120**

1. Discuss menu _____➔_____

2. Decorations _____➔ ➔_____

3. Assign cooking responsibilities _____➔_____

4. _____

5. _____

6. _____

Could you create an implementation plan from the meeting discussion?

What	Who	When	Outcome
Get catering bids	MG	1/23	Cost approved

Reflection:

How much of the meeting was value-added to my work? (review tic marks) _____

_____

What was the labor cost of the meeting? _____

Did the value of the meeting justify the cost?_____My participation? _____

_____

Was the agenda realistic?_____Was the time allowed adequate? _____

Did the participants leave understanding the implementation plan? _____

_____

Could the work have been done better by a small focus group (2–3 people)_____

Ahead of time: Prepare the members (as few as possible to represent the parties involved with the issue) for the fact that they will be using a new approach and focus primarily on one topic; be sure there is a whiteboard or flipchart and pens for drawing.

Using principles of A3 problem solving, a meeting leader would conduct a meeting with the following format:

1. Identify a meeting leader (who understands the A3 process).
2. Introduce members (representing the parties affected by the process/problem).
3. Define the process of a lean meeting and proceed.
    - Define a single issue on which to focus.
    - Assign responsibility of drawing on the board to one member.
    - Have one member draw a paper copy as you progress.

The lean meeting leader (with the group) will:

1. Establish how the work happens now (have assigned person draw on the whiteboard).
2. Determine the problems (go around the table and have each of the affected parties include their concerns) and add where these problems occur on the drawing as storm clouds.
3. Analyze those problems to determine the root cause.
    a. Ask five whys.
4. Determine and draw a target condition on which each affected party agrees.
5. Agree on countermeasures.
6. Create a realistic implementation plan to assign accountability for tasks.
    a. What's going to happen?
    b. Who will do it?
    c. When will it be complete?
    d. What's the expected outcome of each task?
7. Establish date/time/place to reconvene and report results of implementation plan.
8. Design a test of the plan.
9. Get approval of implementation plan and test.
10. Use current condition, target condition, implementation plan, and test as minutes of meeting and distribute.
11. Conduct test.
12. Meet again; report results to group and accept or redesign.
13. If satisfied . . . IMPLEMENT!
14. Schedule and conduct follow-up review.

REDESIGNING COMMUNICATION AND HANDOFFS BETWEEN DEPARTMENTS

The A3 process and documentation format provide an objective boundary tool to communicate issues between departments or functions. Because blaming does not enter the dialogue when evaluating broken work, communication between departments and agencies is fair, clear, and easy to understand and always leads to better relationships. When venturing out of one's realm of influence, it is important to engage members of the other team *early* in the A3 process to declare an accurate current condition from which joint improvement efforts can proceed.

Risk, errors, and waste often occur at the handoff of patients from one caregiver or department to another. Efficient work for A3 thinkers involves examining and jointly creating a bulletproof handoff process.

JUSTIFYING CAPITAL BUDGET REQUESTS

As the responsibility for prudent spending in healthcare becomes more acute, a tool like the A3 document is essential to guarantee that dollars are wisely spent. The document provides administrators who approve the purchase with the necessary data to form the best decision. When requests are made on A3 documents, administrators may review and compare requests quickly, with confidence that proper preparation has been made. Because of the in-depth evaluation process, the A3 may also reveal objectively to a requestor if the purchase is *not* justifiable.

JUSTIFYING STAFFING CHANGES

As with purchase requests, staffing changes can be examined and justified using the A3 process. When this degree of inspection of staffing occurs, many other problems associated with the best use of staff commonly come to the forefront and expose creative improvement options.

DESIGNING WORK SPACES

Recent interest by architects in using lean concepts for the design of structures and spaces that better support work offer a real opportunity for improving safety, quality, and economy in healthcare. When considering the part that new and remodeled construction plays in capital budgets, cost benefits from this sector could be remarkable. Consider using a plan, such as the one in Figure 6–1 to create an ideal medical center.

One consideration: Improving the processes of work before embarking on new construction or remodeling can save buckets of money and improve employee satisfaction. The A3 process creates a language of value for the staff to communicate current problems with the work environment and suggest strategic ideas for a better place to work. While designers and architects have always queried staff about making improvements, the staff has not always possessed the tools to answer with the most specific information. This process creates the understanding of work that enhances the dialogue.

REPORTING IMPROVEMENTS

Documentation of improvement for reporting to hospital administration and board directors, as well as regulatory agencies, is enhanced with a consistent, recognizable tool. The breakdown of information included on the A3 comprises exactly the points that regulators look for when judging an organization's effectiveness in the improvement of safety and quality of care. When A3s on work units are collectively stored in a centrally-located, three-ring binder, examiners can easily access and visualize real improvements on their walking surveys.

PROJECT PLANNING

Projects can be strategically planned and communicated (and changed and updated fluidly) using value stream maps and A3 problem-solving reports as core documents. From the initial understanding of the current work and design of the future

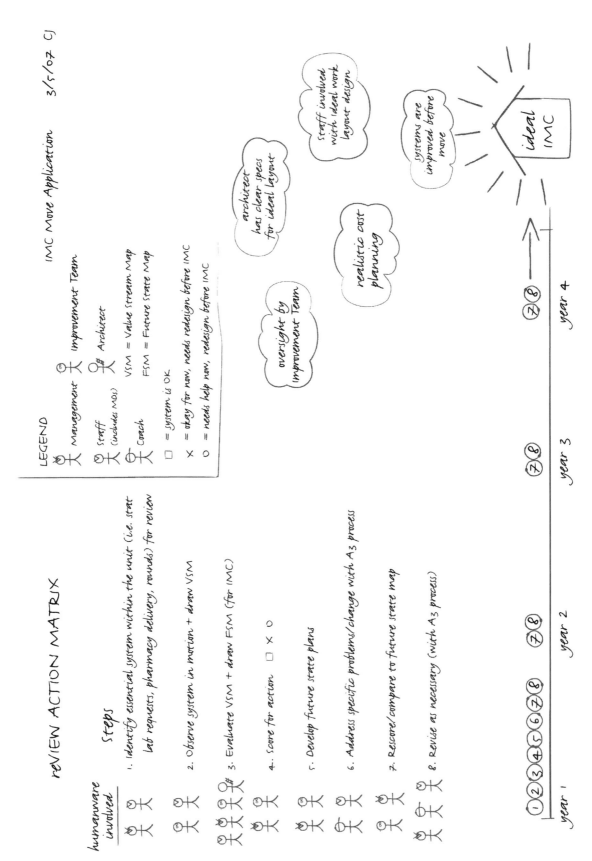

Figure 6-1. Possible A3 action matrix for workspace redesign

state, to the last data comparison, the simple, graphic diagrams illustrate the progress of any project. Using the A3 process in meetings to articulate the issues and justify the concerns and participation of stakeholders involved with the project sets a foundation of common purpose and understanding, communicated with graphic simplicity.

A report of the project work is easy to read and follow. Jump ahead and imagine the project is complete. From top to bottom the document stack progresses like this:

1. On the top of the stack resides the *current state map*. Objectively drawn from direct observation and validated by the working staff for accuracy with data to substantiate variances in occurrences of the process, the map clarifies for the reader everything currently understood about the way this process of work really happens now from a high level view.

2. Once the current state is evaluated and validated, the people doing the work are also involved with developing the *future state map*. This map serves as the beacon that leads the team to the work to which it aspires. The map can be refined as new learning occurs (and it will) during the process, but it will define from the beginning the anticipated goal for a given time, using specified human and fiscal resources. This creates a future-state vision of what can be done to move the work closer to Ideal in a realistic timeframe. It may involve changes in flow or the details of work within the process boxes that will eliminate waste and add value to the patient or customer. The goal will be to improve the quality of the service or product and the reliability of the process. Another significant objective is to make the improvement by redesigning the work, not by increasing FTEs or making unnecessary purchases.

3. Next in the stack is the *future state plan*. This builds and records the accountability for steps that must occur to move the work from the current state to the future state. It will include *what* needs to happen; identified as the problems that will be addressed using the

A3 problem-solving method, *who* will be responsible for each of those improvement activities, anticipation of *when* each of the A3s will be complete, and a clear expectation of the improvement in the value stream that will be realized by the efforts.

4. As work through the future state plan progresses, each A3 will be added to the stack, culminating in a record of all the work that has occurred in the time defined in the future state plan. See Figure 6-2.

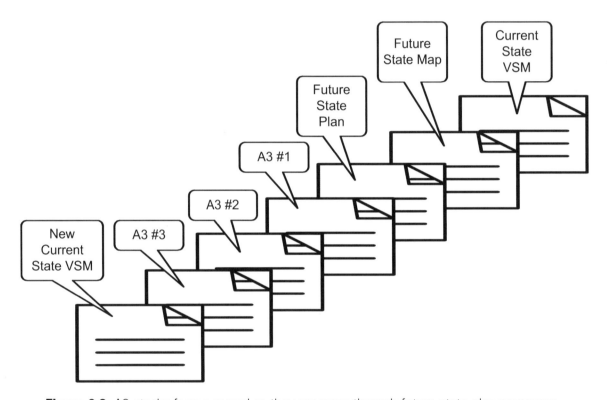

Figure 6-2. A3 stacks form a record as they progress through future state plan processes.

5. At the date designated on the future state map a *new current state map* is created and comparative data collected. At this time, the team reviews the work recorded on the A3s and the two maps to measure how close they came to what was anticipated in the future state vision. The accumulated knowledge and clear-cut improvements prepare the team for the next step—the development of the next future state map. Thus, the project planning can be iterative and continuous until satisfaction is achieved.

From staff to management to regulatory agencies, documentation of projects using this method is easy to review and approve, requires less report writing, and creates more capacity for even more improvements.

SHARING THE LEARNING WITH THE REST OF THE ORGANIZATION AND THE HEALTHCARE INDUSTRY

Anytime work is standardized, the results of that work are easier to report and share across the organization. That includes the work of changing and improving processes. From department to department and from hospital to hospital industry-wide learning can occur when all use a simple and common method. A3s can be scanned, photographed, or converted to electronic images for presentations and archiving. Units can store their paper A3s in a binder that can be reviewed by staff or used as a routine update tool in staff meetings. Managers can review and share improvements that may have applications for other departments with other managers. Chapter 8 elaborates on how to share the work electronically.

7

Coaching A3 Problem Solving in a Learning Organization

EFFECTIVE LEARNING

Effective learning is really what A3 thinking and problem solving is all about—learning what we can about the way work currently transpires to develop a new way to work. As is demonstrated by Figure 7–1, the most effective adult learning method is *one-on-one*. This validates Toyota's success with coaching as a requisite of problem solving. Notice also that the second most effective method is *learning by doing*. A3 problem solving, which

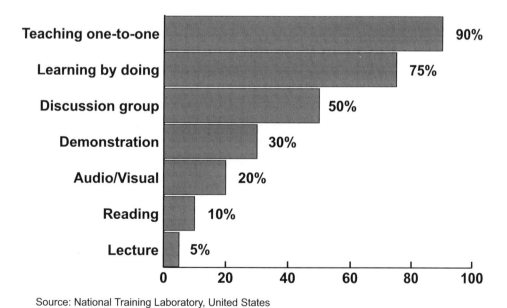

**Effective Learning:
% of Knowledge Retained after Completion**

Source: National Training Laboratory, United States

Figure 7–1. One-to-one teaching accounts for 90 percent of effective learning in the United States.

must always be done in a safe environment of experimentation, based on observation and *supported* by a coach, embraces those two most effective learning styles. But what exactly constitutes coaching?

COACHING

... the art of inspiring, energizing, and facilitating the performance, learning, and development of a team member.

Each word in this definition is key:

- **art**—Although there is a science to coaching, coaching is an art, in the sense that when practiced with excellence, attention to technique seems unnecessary: The coach is fully engaged with the player, and the process of coaching becomes a dance between two people, conversationally moving in complete harmony and partnership. At this point, the intelligence, intuition, and imagination of the coach become a valuable contribution—rather than being interference for the player.

- **inspiring**—Coaching helps the player to unlock his or her true potential through raising awareness, inspiring new ideas, and encouraging creativity.

- **energizing**—Coaching involves energizing the player through effective communication, soliciting suggestions, and building a can-do attitude.

- **facilitating**—This implies that the player has the capacity to have an insight or creative idea and to think something through for him/herself.

- **performance**—The intention to improve performance (i.e., to achieve greater effectiveness or efficiency of the player) should drive anything a coach says or does.

- **learning**—This refers to a broader domain—how to approach a task or master a new technology. Looking beyond immediate objectives, the future performance of the organization depends on learning.

- **development**—This refers to personal growth and greater self-awareness.[1]

Leaders as Coaches

The implementation of TPS/Lean concepts in any organization requires a shift, not only in the way leadership assigns responsibility of work units to self-manage, but also in the *daily work* of managers and directors. Rather than directing or managing work in progress and problems that arise, their position shifts to a facilitating role. Herein lies one of the most powerful features of the A3 thinking and A3 problem-solving practices. Rather than receiving complaints and dealing with problems in conventional meetings or from a "command and control" position, the lean leader coaches pertinent staff through the A3 process to solve problems at the source of those complaints. Instead of fixing problems delivered to his/her desk, the true coach observes, listens, and asks questions of involved staff to determine the root cause of any troublesome work, leading to a solution created by the staff.

A3 problem solving becomes easier and more logical with every activity in which it is used; its applicability to endless areas of work becomes apparent quickly. The rewarding work of coaching staff to arrive at a level of comfort with this method of structured problem solving requires attention to the elements of effective coaching. Coaching should not be confused with mentoring . . . this is not just *listening* but rather, *active listening*, to which the response is *active questioning* to help the problem solver discover the root cause of the issue at hand. Essentially, leaders need to practice the art of coaching regularly in order to hone this fine skill.

Administrative Roles

While anyone with the time and motivation to help people think and take initiatives to change their work can fill the role of an

---

1. Excerpted from 1000ventures.com by Vadim Kotelnikov as adapted from *Effective Coaching: Lessons from the Coach's Coach* by Myles Downey. New York: Texere, 2003.

effective coach, the job naturally suits the work of middle managers. It requires rearranging traditional managerial work and a real commitment to look at one's own daily duties differently. As simple as this might sound, it requires ego strength and a willingness to stretch personal boundaries. The transition from traditional management to truly effective coach/leader involves three keys recognized by Toyota senior leaders. They include:

1. *Go see*. This means leaving the office area to go see what's really happening out there. Called *"gemba* walks" in industry, a regular, nonthreatening visit to see how processes really support the work (or not) keeps a leader informed and the staff enthused.

2. *Ask "Why?"* Again, in a typical "command and control" work environment, workers may perceive questioning (rightfully so) as a threat. In lean leadership asking *why* shows an expression of sincerity or an attempt to understand how and why things happen the way they do. The motive for asking *why* is never punitive; it just brings the team of coaches and participants closer to understanding the issue.

3. *Show respect*. Coaches need to structure their visits and questions to demonstrate respect for the experience and knowledge that workers have achieved in preparing for and attending to their assigned work. Regarding workers as the "resident experts" in their job area will be invaluable in revealing detailed opportunities and in garnering buy-in for change.

Coaches cannot instill *A3 thinking* in their workers if they don't know and use the tools themselves. Coaches especially need to use A3 thinking and documents in everyday work at every level of the organization, to establish credibility with staff. This practice maximizes the power of the process and extracts the most return from the investment. Soon, opportunities to use A3 thinking and the A3 reporting tools will skyrocket as coaches and workers gain more experience with this method.

Although Toyota and other manufacturers use the A3 document for reporting many other activities, the A3 problem-solving method enables coaches to offer objective direction and focus to a problem. The first activity involves prompting the worker to define the issue through the eyes of the customer/patient; the coach parlays the first gift to the worker—putting the perspective where it belongs. Without a coach many people tend to see the problem through their own eyes and may miss much of the value that a second, objective view can help reveal.

Communicating the initial statement of the issue to other workers is one of the basic strengths of the tool, and coaches can use this to garner staff cooperation toward designing a better way to work. Likewise with every step, visualizing each logical move on the road to improvement supersedes the customary verbal discussion of a problem. The coach has the ability to take the A3 document from worker to worker, department to department, and to busy administrators, presenting the situation in a simple format. Consider the game Gossip, where one person whispers something in the ear of the person next to him or her, and the message is passed along. The fun of the game is hearing the final rendition of the message, which almost never resembles the original words. The traveling A3 standardizes the report of the improvement work being done.

The facile coach, with document and pencil in hand, can quickly include input from those involved with the work, from the bottom to the top of the organizational chain. Expecting busy caregivers, or any worker to stop his or her routine work to initiate and complete the redesign of a troublesome process, is unrealistic in most work environments. The role of the coach to respond when a concern is raised is paramount to successful problem solving. Students of the Toyota Production System understand the authority of the worker to "stop the line" when a defect in production is recognized. While that may not be literally possible in the care of a patient, the principle of addressing a problematic event, *as close in time and person* as possible, proves vital when endeavoring to move closer to Ideal.

In order to offer this kind of responsiveness, a strong structure of coaches with time to support the frontline staff is necessary. In the planning stages of implementing lean and particularly A3 problem solving, it's crucial to the success of the program to recognize potential coaches. Initially, the people who already have the responsibilities for quality enhancement, process improvement, staff education, and organizational operations make likely candidates for A3 coaches. Coaches should come from existing positions, without hiring anyone new, but the process almost always necessitates restructuring their work.

As work units are introduced to A3 problem solving, the managers, directors, local unit educators, and team leaders must be included in training. Redefining their roles to shift from the current state to A3 thinking and coaching can pose the most difficult leap in changing the culture of an organization, but herein lies the power to move this simple and practical method through the organization. The important message to send to these future lean leaders is: They will not have *extra* work, but a more satisfying way to perform the work in which they are currently involved. Enthusiasm spreads throughout the front line when an organization's leadership speaks the same language and respects workers in the same voice.

Continuing to develop informal leaders as coaches enriches the structure and potential to provide assistance to bright workers who recognize problems in the course of work. These informal leaders include the confident and reasonable workers who thrive in their daily jobs and earn the respect of their peers for the management of their own work. These everyday role models are essential in coaching A3 problem solving with their peers. Imagine, after 57 years, Toyota still practices TPS daily; its coaching philosophy and commitment has enabled the staff to deliver the quality and success that the organization boasts annually.

Coaching structures should include not only internal coaches, but access to external coaching as well. It's important for every coach to have a *sensei* or coach with whom he or she can consult when a new approach is required or a set of fresh eyes is needed to evaluate the unforeseen. Building support at every level is critical to stay fresh and objective. Learning from the ever-expanding applications and experiences of other similar organizations will be well worth the effort and dollars spent when an outside coach is employed.

Internal coaches are resources from an existing organization, trained and recognized at every level to support and promote A3 thinking. It is generally not necessary to hire new staff, although organizing the work of current staff to include coaching time is critical. The beginning of this process can create the greatest challenge for coaches, but a couple of concepts can facilicate developing these valuable positions from current job descriptions.

The first of these concepts, and one alluded to earlier, states: *Employees will not have extra work, but a more satisfying way to perform the work in which they are currently involved.* That means that the coach should take the next problem that comes to his/her desk and tackle it *this way*: If it requires sharing the problem at a meeting, getting input from peers, or observing to better understand the current condition, the steps of the A3 process apply. In this practical, on-the-job approach lies the potential to convert from the silo approach to addressing issues, to a learning, *thinking* organization that solves problems together.

The second concept refers to *reinvesting the time saved with the first activity into more problem solving.* Without fail, if workers adhere faithfully to the A3 problem-solving structure, worker time will be optimized and capacity increased. When this occurs with a full- or part-time coach, who likely has other responsibilities in his or her daily work, the tendency is to give this person even more responsibilities. This issues a death warrant to a coach's morale and ability to succeed! However, if coaches can reinvest that rescued, non-value added time into more problem solving, even greater system improvements can be realized quickly and with the enthusiasm of all the people doing the work; and successful and timely problem solving strongly motivates staff to look for even more processes to improve.

Identifying the right coaches within an organization will likely include some full-time coaches and some employees who can be assigned part-time hours to do the job. The essential key to their success is that they are prepared and recognized as coaches; that they are given the resource time to fulfill the task of coaching; and that a reliable system of issue reporting, coaching, and follow-up is established.

Initially, coaches will not only guide staff in solving problems, but also help them recognize opportunities to use A3 problem solving and how to use coaches as a resource. In conjunction with the value stream map and other lean tools, A3 problem solving becomes an integral part of the communication of problems in work as well as the bright ideas for improving it. Coaches who use those tools to guide the vision of staff toward an Ideal state find great personal satisfaction in their jobs and will enjoy assisting others toward these common goals.

COACHING VERSUS CONVENTIONAL CLASSROOM EDUCATION

A3 problem solving is perfectly designed with a structured tool and logical thinking to be enhanced by an experienced coach. While the principles and concepts can be taught in a classroom setting and are easy to demonstrate with examples, coaching actual work improvement in a one-on-one or small group setting creates a bulletproof adult learning environment. The talented coach uses succinct questions to guide members of a small group to teach each other what they know. The coach has the advantage of developing a relationship of mutual respect in an informal environment that creates comfort with questioning and extracts the personal knowledge of the worker/workers. This environment enables the team to deeply understand the work and elicit suggestions for improvement.

Responding to requests for coaching and scheduling can pose a challenge in the initial implementation of A3 problem solving. It is essential that those coaches are properly prepared (i.e., experienced in both A3 thinking and adult coaching) and that a system is developed for certain access to coaching. Organizations approach this challenge in different ways. Some may use a written log in which problems can be reported (and always read by assigned coaches) with faith that a response will be reliable and prompt. Some departments use e-mail for communication between workers and coaches. One outpatient diagnostic clinic stores a pad of blank A3 forms in a clear acrylic file outside the door of the director's office and when a problem arises, the worker fills in as much as he or she can to define the issue and initial information and leaves it in an adjacent clear acrylic file, labeled "hot A3s." The director can't miss the "hot A3" in the box as she enters her office, and she reviews and assigns the A3 to an available and appropriate coach in the applicable department. This ensures that the director is notified of the problem, and while it may not be necessary for her to coach the problem personally, she can assign the responsibility for completion and stay involved with improving the process. Each department or organization must define the process of responding to a reported problem. Be creative, but be sure to abide by Rule 1: Specify the process clearly!

Scheduling follow-up coaching to an initial session is important to maintain the confidence of the staff and to ensure that the details of the A3 are achieved and evaluated for further possible improvement. Good rapport with the staff and on-site checkups to see how the work is progressing reinforces the learning and inspires close scrutiny of the improvement to ensure success.

Combining classroom education, practical application of theory to real work, and individual coaching creates a model that appeals to adult learners. Coaching allows the learner to clarify any points that he or she may have overlooked in class and to be guided through a practical activity of improvement, whereas a classroom setting alone cannot provide this interaction.

As a continuous activity, coaching A3 problem solving creates the atmosphere and habit of improvement as opposed to a classroom activity, which is confined to a set beginning and end. The true learning organization recognizes opportunities in every activity of work to make a change for the better. The use of a structure such as A3 problem solving makes the process of learning consistent and methodical. The role of the coach in maintaining the momentum of transformation can't be underestimated.

The coach must remember to allow the person being coached to work through the problem him or herself. The coach's role is *not* to resolve the issue, but to challenge the worker to think and discover—questioning him or her to devise ways to make the service more productive and efficient sparks the worker's creative thought process. Asking questions like, "What hasn't been done *yet*?" to suggest an overlooked improvement, or an opportunity to expand a line of thought, greatly motivates the learner to think for him or herself.

The observation, listening, and questioning inherent in both value stream maps and A3s make them ideal coaching tools

THE GRAPHIC COACH

One factor with the potential to stop some problem solvers in their tracks is the request to draw the current condition. Some employees may say, "But I'm no artist." The point of drawing spaghetti diagrams and arrows and stick people in the current condition and target condition, however, is to visualize loops in work—those obstructions worked around and reworked because of weak processes. Renoir and Picasso likely wouldn't consider this art!

Many studies have been done on the effectiveness of graphics in problem solving. Creating a sketch moves the problem solving from our linear, calculating left brain to the creative conceptual activities in our right brain, where our best problem solving occurs. This is one of the most powerful aspects of A3 problem solving, it forces us to use the *whole brain*.[2]

Because many people are less familiar with graphic expression, the coach needs to be comfortable with simple graphics. Using a preestablished basic set of icons (see the example in Appendix D, page 143) and creating an elementary legend when new icons are introduced, makes the drawing activity fun and the result evocative.

When one coaches problem solving, it's important to coax the worker to create the initial drawing, even if the first rendition is crude and hard to read. Having the right materials on

---

2. Pink, D. *A Whole New Mind.* New York: Penguin Group, 2006.

hand makes drawing more comfortable. Those materials may include a whiteboard, hung on a horizontal orientation and supplied with fresh erasable markers of a few different colors. Any piece of paper, or an A3 form, and a pencil with a stout eraser works as well. Uncomfortable sketchers always seem to make their drawings small but with a little encouragement to use the whole available space, almost everyone can depict movement of people and products, information and obstacles. Using different colors to indicate information flow, patient flow, and worker flow can make even a complicated mess of work easy to understand in an image. A group of people can transition, from a few frustrated efforts, to a collective understanding and a common agreement of how a piece of work happens, simply through drawing, erasing, and finally completing a sketch of a work process. When this group starts adding its specific storm clouds (in red) to the first current condition drawing, heads may start nodding, as the mental wheels begin to spin. When identifying those storm clouds, which obstruct the ability to perform value-added work, an effective coach involves every individual team member to include all concerns.

When getting the team to draw with a pencil, don't forget to worship the eraser! The power of using a pencil (or whiteboard) is that misconceptions can be corrected on the spot. No revising a report, no delay.

Even if all of the early drawings don't make it to the final A3, save them to reflect on later. Reviewing several renditions of A3s used to correct a complex problem is fun, rewarding, and quick: Just spread them out on a table or hang them on a wall.

Some slick electronic tools available for drawing A3s offer many occasions for getting clever with electronic conversions for data management, sharing images by e-mail, and embellishing presentations. A3s can be converted to electronic formats later, but the first activity of pushing the pencil proves productive and liberating. Coaches should encourage problem solvers to become comfortable with drawing by hand.

An effective coach (think of the beloved sports coaches you know) becomes a mentor and gains the respect of the people with whom he or she works. When a good coach serves as a role model and acknowledges staff success, the benefits are countless.

EDUCATION/TRAINING

The Toyota Production System, and particularly A3 problem solving, do not involve weeks or even hours of theoretical study in advance of beginning the application. In fact, the best way to learn A3s is a combination of a short lecture to understand the method, the goals, and how to choose something to work on; real life application of the method as the learning occurs; and being coached in that application.

Quick learning may be obtained with direct observation accompanied by an observation activity in which each participant chooses something he or she finds troublesome, followed by a guided observation.

Building on the observation activity, the next lesson teaches the fundamentals of value stream mapping and understanding the *flow* of a particular process (again, the subject chosen by the participant or the team). As the individual or the team is coached, any errors or omissions in understanding and any missed interpretation of the process can be mitigated by observing again to clarify. This ensures that as the participants *learn by doing*, their work on the chosen problem is being validated; theories and motivations are questioned to acquire deep understanding; and a collegial learning relationship is fostered within the team and with the coach.

The third assignment involves collecting data to understand the process more deeply. Simple but accurate data will *objectively* point to the areas of the process where the greatest delays occur between essential steps and the most significant variability in the process. Those areas reflect the best opportunity to identify specific problems that can be addressed with A3 problem solving.

Once the big picture of the process is understood with the value stream map and data and the improved process is projected on a future state map, a plan to improve the process is developed and A3s are assigned to achieve the goals of the plan. In each of these classes, the practical *learning by doing* and the coaching sessions to review and enhance the work done from class to class are every bit as important as the lecture information.

Subsequent short lectures can be taught to familiarize participants, first with the left side of the A3 (and of course the assignment is to initiate an A3 and complete the left side on a topic *meaningful to the participant*), and then the right side. This process can't be rushed. The left side of the A3 may create a challenge in the beginning, usually because the participant chooses too broad or too big an issue. When the class shares the initial left-side work and individuals expose their own struggles with this new process and with the problematic work in which they are engaged, everyone begins to learn from each other. Covering every part of the A3 in the training sessions is essential to successful implementation.

Sharing A3s and the Associated Learning

8

One of the advantages of using structured tools for problem solving is the ability to share the learning and improvements in a common language. Using a standard methodology, understood across the organization, makes it possible to create uniform electronic and hard copy reporting tools from the paper drawn documents.

Electronic versions of hand-drawn value stream maps and A3 problem-solving documents can be used in presentations, cross-organizational reporting, general communications of improvement work by e-mail, and as justification for formal proposals. Each of the A3 examples included in Chapter 9 of this book was originally created with a pencil on paper. The illustrator for this book converted them to a digital format.

Another advantage of creating electronic images is the ability to store them in a secure or open web-based forum. Examples of options for creating and storing work well done are discussed in the following section.

eVSM/eA3

In a learning organization, the development and use of the A3 document for problem solving, creating lean meetings, and communicating a new way to look at work leads naturally to the necessity to share those accomplishments. Electronic images of the documents create concise versions of the work for printing, sending via e-mail, and projecting as overheads in educational and reporting presentations. The variety of applications of these documents will expand with practice, demand,

and experience. This book was illustrated with *eVSM/eA3*.[1] eVSM is simple "drag & drop" software that supports lean practitioners in drawing, sharing, and analyzing value stream maps and A3 reports.

Value stream maps and A3s are developed in the software by using a comprehensive library of icons for lean healthcare, services, and manufacturing applications. The library is expandable to suit the development of even more articulate reports that can be customized to suit every process situation. Icons for healthcare workers and patients can even indicate emotions, representing them with a smile, neutral, or unhappy expression. See Figure 8–1.

Figure 8–1. Happy, neutral, and sad icons.

Straight arrows can be curved and stretched to show movement of people, products, and information. Lines can be solid or perforated in several densities (see Figure 8–2). And all lines and icons can be colored in the standard electronic selection. This flexibility creates thousands of options for separating information to create an easy-to-follow, articulate sketch with a simple click of the mouse.

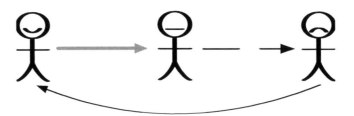

Figure 8–2. Lines can be straight, curved, or perforated, in a variety of densities and colors.

The capability for creating templates makes it easy to create several iterations of drawings without starting from scratch.

---

1. Patel D, and Ranpuria, H. *eVSM/eA3*. 2006

This can be particularly valuable in situations where the same or similar activity has been looked at in many locations. Making the small but important changes to enunciate the nuances from department to department is easy to modify, using one initial drawing template (e.g., looking at the admission process in several different office practices or the inventory stocking process from department to department).

Sometimes a value stream map is very high level, perhaps a view from 100,000 feet, from which several more detailed maps will be developed before problem solving begins. The templates and "drag and drop" behavior of this kind of tool saves time and confusion in support of this kind of work.

Storm clouds have been designed as text boxes. The storm cloud itself can be made in a color that contrasts with the sketch of the work, which nicely separates the flow from the identified problems.

The eVSM eLearning site (*www.evsm.com/help*) includes a learning path that allows practitioners to get started easily and learn the software in a modular fashion.

Value stream maps and A3s created with this software can be saved as PDFs. The Share module on the eLearning site shows how maps and reports can be shared with people who do not have any special software.

The program also enables the user to calculate formulas from the data acquired. The Analyze module on the eLearning site shows how to add data to the icons and analyze and store it in a spreadsheet.

Logging improvement activities and collating information for reports are easily performed with electronic data repositories like the Improvement Marquee® discussed below, and the inclusion of the graphic content of the A3 enhances the clarity of the data stored. Building on the value of the graphic features of the A3, the replication in storage, communicating, and reporting further enhance the features of the A3 process.

ELECTRONIC A3 STORAGE AND SHARING

Almost immediately, when adopting A3s in a healthcare setting, it will become apparent that improvements are occurring simultaneously and therein lie great opportunities for sharing what is learned. Storage of the paper A3s on the units in a central location works well for local use, but the opportunities to extend the benefits outside the original location pose a bigger challenge. However, as A3s become the method for reporting changes at meetings, reference to A3 successes can be followed up and visually reviewed with a data repository to store them and share them as needed

Data storage of improvements should *at least* include the issue, the root cause, the target vision, and a contact person to reach for details. Measurement of the occurrence, cost, and quality of the improved work also proves valuable in weighing the importance of the activity to the organization.

Lean Healthcare West (*www.leanhealthcarewest.com*) has developed a free, secure web-based data repository. The Improvement Marquee® allows organizations to share A3 documents internally or to select A3s, one-by-one, to share on a public website.

Administrator functions can be assigned to specific individuals who will enter, edit, and delete A3 reports within an organization's secure account. *Read only* passwords can be assigned to staff, administration, boards of directors, or with whomever the organization chooses to communicate improvement progress.

This method and the real A3s contributed for public viewing can be accessed at *www.improvementmarquee.com*.

Case Studies

9

These 11 examples have been selected from hundreds of A3s to offer a snapshot of different improvements and demonstrate a variety of sources of waste (*mudas*) and violations of the 4 Rules in Use. In the summary of each graphic A3 you will see how the problem was recognized and how the improvement was initiated.

Some of these case studies saved considerable money, some improved safety and quality, and some made work leaner and less frustrating for the people doing the work.

This section serves to inspire imaginations to adapt the A3 process to various settings and to a constellation of situations.

Note: The illustrations in this chapter will demonstrate how specific problems for A3s are recognized and relate to a value stream map (VSM). Recall that the VSM is a high-level view of a process and the A3 is a focused look at a specific problem within the value stream. A3s are the perfect tool for tackling the specific problems that contribute to variance in the data in a process box.

CONCLUSION

Hopefully this text inspires you to use the simple and reliable A3 Problem Solving method in your daily work. Like any change of routine it takes practice to realize the potential of A3s, but you will start to see the power of the process in your first activity.

CASE STUDY 1: ED CHART ORGANIZATION

Reducing Accounts Receivable (AR) Days from Emergency Department (ED) Charges

The first A3 includes an associated VSM from which it was recognized. This will illustrate the relationship between the two process tools.

This issue was brought to the improvement team by a CFO who was concerned that the accounts receivable (AR) days for charges from the emergency department (ED) took longer than the national average. His request was that the team observe the billing/payment process and decipher why it took so long to collect for outpatient emergency charges.

Figure 9–1 shows the VSM that was created for this purpose.

The team visited the billing department staff to validate the data. Staff members explained that preparing a bill took only a matter of a few minutes if the corresponding chart was completely coded. They suggested the team observe the coding activities in the medical records department to determine why some charts came to them uncoded and why they resided so long in the coding department.

From evaluation of the data, the "coding" process box revealed a large variation in time to code an ED chart, with the low being 1 day and the high 34. Because the "coding" box was furthest upstream in the billing process, it had a high likelihood of affecting the processes downstream, which further validated the suggestions of the billing department to look at coding activities.

As part of their routine, the coders kept a hard-copy list of the charts that were incomplete (not enough information to code charges), and the dates on which they were received. It was easy to recognize the aging charts. Closer evaluation of those records revealed that the greatest sources of missing information came from the absence of the doctor's final dictation as well as incomplete nursing notes. The coders suggested that the evaluation team observe the emergency department, and the journey continued further upstream, out of the billing area.

When the investigators questioned the nurses about how they determined if a chart was complete upon a patient's discharge, a complex and uncertain system was described. Included in the description was the responsibility of the *charge nurse* (the person least involved with the direct care) to scan each chart before allowing it to be disassembled. When asked why this valuable clinical person (the highest paid nurse in the department) was checking other nurses' and doctors' work, the explanation was simple ... they were

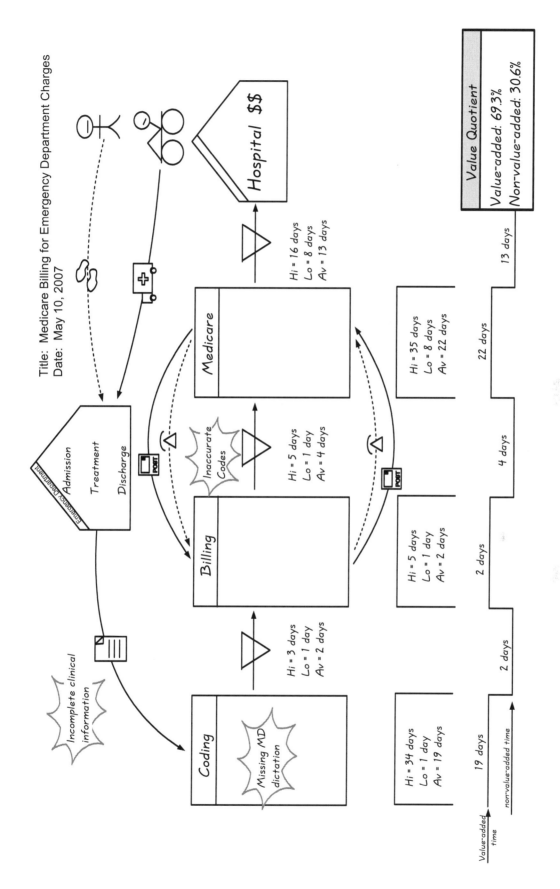

Figure 9-1. Medicare billing for emergency department charges. See Appendices C and D for symbol definitions

missing too many charges, and charts were incomplete. When asked why a chart sometimes would be sent without complete nursing documentation, the nurses explained that sometimes the doctors hid the charts, and they couldn't find them before they went home at the end of the shift. Also, most saw the accountability for *completeness* as a responsibility of the charge nurse, not one that they should own individually.

The interviewed doctors answered similarly: They sometimes couldn't dictate a record of care after discharge because the nurses sometimes hid the charts! While this was beginning to sound like an episode of the Keystone Cops, it was real and created confusion, potential errors, and omissions in care and billing, not to mention bad feelings between staff members.

The improvement team elected to watch chart flow through the ED to try to pinpoint areas of concern, and this was identified as the issue of the first A3 (see Fig. 9-2). When the current condition was drawn on the A3, the staff began to see the picture clearly. There was no way to know where the chart was at any given time, when the patient was in the department or outside during diagnostic exams. There were many locations and many caregivers hand-carrying the chart from bedside to workstation with no designated destination for the information.

The staff reviewed the problems (*storm clouds*) associated with the current condition and heard the doctors voice their frustration with not being able to find charts. Doctors were relying on their memories to recall which patients required dictation after a busy day and expressed fear of failure when dictating after the day of care. It was easy to recognize that the root cause of the problem was *no designated location for charts during a patient's visit to the ED*. At any given time, the patient might be in his or her room, in the department, or out of the department receiving diagnostic studies, and there was no indicator of his or her progress through the visit (or if the chart was with him or her). All communication was face to face, sometimes with many faces to determine the status and next steps of a patient's course of care. This affected not only the physicians, but also all ED and consulting staff and, of course, extended the time of the patient's visit and potentially delayed treatment.

Once the root cause of the problem was understood, it was easy to visualize a target condition. Everyone agreed that they needed a method of tracking the chart and progress of care. It was further agreed that a simple row of clearly marked, differently colored boxes, mounted on the top of the nurses' station counter would be an easy way to test the notion. The ward clerk and a member of the improvement team agreed to spray paint seven chart-sized, cardboard boxes a different color, and all staff agreed to use the color-coded system for 1 week. This ensured that by the time the chart arrived at the final box, all information was noted, and the physician could dictate a timely and accurate note.

The *role of the charge nurse in monitoring charting* arose as a problem several times, and the team agreed on a second countermeasure. A checklist was developed with a large, easy-to-read font and checkboxes to indicate completion for the vital recording that the charge nurse had formerly validated. This list was placed on the cover of every chart, and the staff agreed to initial in the box, when the work was recorded. This enabled anyone to see, at a glance, what parts of the chart were complete, and it allowed the charge nurse to focus on more valuable work.

At the conclusion of the test, the staff agreed wholeheartedly that this simple process had removed frustration, redundant searching, and delay from their work. More permanent light wooden boxes (color coded, of course) replaced the paper boxes for little investment.

The follow-up, 4 months later, showed more impressive results than anyone had imagined. The staff was happy with the process, and the AR days in the emergency department were reduced from 91 to 42 days! Although on this A3 the reduction in wasted activities in the coding and billing departments or Medicare's office were not measured, fixing this problem way upstream certainly affected the people who touched the chart downstream and more savings of time were certainly realized in those areas.

More significantly, it was impossible to measure the inevitable improvement in care performed *on demand* with the time captured by a better process.

MUDAS (sources of waste): Confusion, Motion, Waiting, Defects, Overproduction

ROOT CAUSE: There was no system to identify where the chart was at any time during the patient's visit in the ED.

COUNTERMEASURE: Create transparent system for locating chart and indicating progress of patient in ED.

Relationship to the 4 RULES IN USE:

- **Rule 1:** Activities of Work Clearly Specified. (*No process defined for chart information flow.*)

- **Rule 2:** Connections. (*Communication and handoffs of patient information was haphazard and often required many encounters to locate information.*)

ISSUE *Medical record submitted to coding department without MD dictation after patient is discharged.*

BACKGROUND

MD's work 12 hour shifts, work eight shifts/month.
RNs work 12 hour shifts.
Charge nurse on each shift.
Ward clerk from 6 am until midnight.

Average accounts receivable days: 91
In one month there were 23 charts without MD dictation.

CURRENT CONDITION

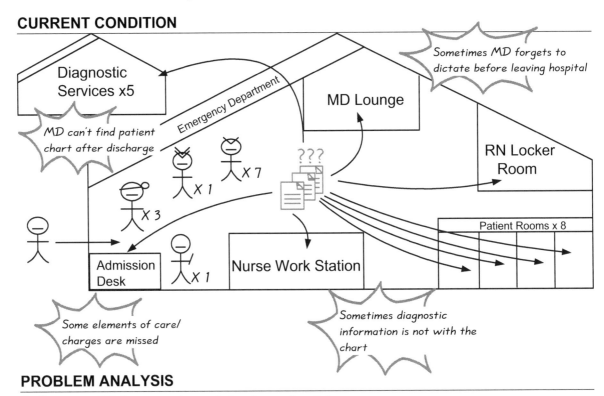

PROBLEM ANALYSIS

1. *Sometimes MD forgets to dictate before leaving hospital*
    Why? There are many charts to keep track of on a busy shift
        Why? MD relies on memory
            Why? No other system
2. *MD can't find patient chart after discharge*
    Why? Not clear if other staff member is using the chart
        Why? No defined chart location
    Why? Chart not where MD left it
        Why? No assigned location for the patient chart
3. *Sometimes diagnostic information is not with the chart*
    Why? Person responsible for compiling diagnostic information can't find the chart
        Why? No assigned location for the chart when patient returns to ED
4. *Some elements of care/charges are missed*
    Why? MD dictates on a patient that he hasn't seen for days
        Why? Chart goes to coding before MD has dictated on it
            Why? Not always clear if MD has dictated
                Why? No chart completion indicator/checklist

Figure 9–2. Emergency department chart organization.

TARGET CONDITION

Title: ED Chart Organization

TO	Susan
BY	Alicia
DATE	September 1, 2006

All workers know where patient and chart are in the flow of care

MD knows when chart is complete/when patient is discharged

X 7

X 3

New Patient	RN Exam Complete	MD Orders	To Diagnostic Department	From Diagnostic Department	MD Discharge	RN Discharge

Nurse Work Station

COUNTERMEASURES

1. Create designated location for chart.
2. Create a checklist for the front of the chart where each caregiver can acknowledge completion of steps of care.

IMPLEMENTATION PLAN

What	Who	When	Outcome
Order colored boxes	WC	9/5/06	Clear signal of chart location
Inform staff when boxes are installed	CN	9/16/06	Begin new process
Develop charting checklist	CN	9/10/06	Quick reference to completed charting

COST/BENEFIT

Cost	
Cost	$$$
Colored boxes	$35
Staff time	$110
Benefit	$$$
Reduce accounts receivable days	More $$
Improve time to patient care	Quality

TEST

Spray paint cardboard boxes to use for chart steps. Coders evaluate charts for level of completion for 1 week. Evaluate for changes.

FOLLOW UP

January 10, 2007
Accounts receivable days reduced to 42 days.
2 charts without MD dictation Dec. 10–Jan. 10.

CASE STUDY 2: SHOCK TRAUMA ICU MEDICATIONS

This A3 was identified by a clinical pharmacist. It demonstrates improvement in safety and prompt delivery of critical treatment to ICU patients.

The pharmacist observed that during the daily sit-down rounds on the busy trauma unit of this Level 1 trauma center, the charts of all the patients currently on the unit were kept in the rounds room. Several people attended rounds: nursing staff from the unit, attending physicians and residents, the clinical pharmacist, and other appropriate ancillary services representatives. When the discussion of a patient was concluded, physician orders were written and the chart (hard copy) returned to the chart rack, which remained in the room until all patients had been discussed and plans of care adjusted.

Medication orders were discussed with the clinical pharmacist during rounds, but the order did not go to the pharmacy for processing until all charts were returned to the ward clerk at the conclusion of rounds. Each chart was processed from the stack, with no preference unless indicated by someone from the rounds team.

The pharmacist discussed her observations with the attending physicians, ward clerk, and manager of the nursing unit, all of whom concurred that the many steps created delay of medication delivery to the patient. The average turnaround time for new orders in this critical care unit was 4 hours!

The pharmacist also validated the process with other clinical pharmacists in the medical and cardiac ICUs and discovered that the process, although slightly different, suffered the same delays in those critical areas.

This issue, because it involved critical medications given to very ill patients, was one that had high priority for accuracy and close monitoring for safety. The medical director of the ICU agreed to monitor the test and evaluate its effectiveness.

The medical director of the ICU and the pharmacist defined the test, with the agreement of the ICU manager and ward clerk, to be conducted for 1 week. The following test was conducted.

The pharmacist used an available laptop computer during rounds and at the conclusion of the discussion of each patient, when the doctor wrote new medication orders, she entered the orders directly into the electronic order-entry system, and these orders were delivered immediately to the pharmacy for processing. The result was a reduction from the average 4-hour new medication delivery time to the patient to an average of 26 minutes.

In addition to the obvious improvement in delivery time for the patient, the ward clerk and RN who had to check the order were removed from the process. The pharmacist saw each medication order while the physician was still in the room to confirm agreement and safety for the patient. Frustration of the bedside nurses and doctors was reduced, as were interrupting phone calls to the pharmacy.

MUDAS (source of waste): Confusion, Processing, Waiting, Overproduction

ROOT CAUSE: There were too many steps and people required to order medications for the Shock Trauma ICU, resulting in redundant work and delays to the patient.

COUNTERMEASURE: Use available technology to create a simplified, direct connection with the pharmacy. Only the essential steps to the process are retained.

Relationship to the 4 RULES IN USE:

- **Rule 2:** Connections. (*Not all the steps for requesting medications on the Shock Trauma ICU were essential. The nonessential steps created a greater opportunity for medication delay, error, and waste of worker time.*) See Figure 9–3.

ISSUE   *Administration of newly ordered medications delayed after orders are written in rounds in Shock Trauma ICU.*

BACKGROUND

Medication orders are created during rounds meeting, then they are sent to the pharmacy to be filled. Orders are written during/after rounds and then processed by the ward clerk and pharmacy. Average time taking off orders: 31 minutes/chart

CURRENT CONDITION

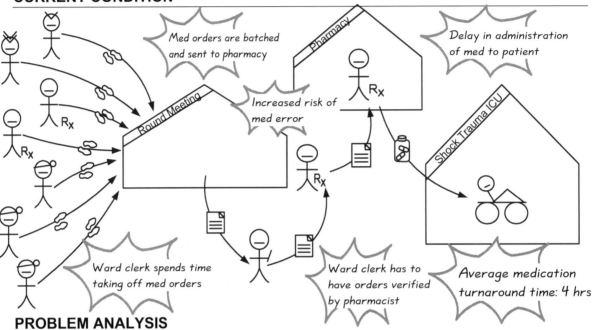

PROBLEM ANALYSIS

1. *Medication orders are batched and create delays in pharmacy*
    Why? *Orders are taken during rounds and given to the ward clerk. They are delivered to the pharmacy when all orders are complete*
2. *Delay in the administration of the medication to the patient*
    Why? *The pharmacy has lots of orders to fill for the Shock Trauma ICU*
        Why? *Orders are done in batches*
3. *Ward clerk spends a lot of time taking off med orders*
    Why? *Many interruptions while taking off orders*
        Why? *The ward clerk is responsible for multiple tasks*
    Why? *Ward clerk has to find pharmacist and have all orders checked*
        Why? *Pharmacist must approve final transcribed order before submission to pharmacy*
            Why? *Standard procedure*
4. *Increased risk for medication error*
    Why? *Many people handle and transcribe the med order*
        Why? *It is given to the ward clerk then back to the pharmacist and then to the pharmacy*

Figure 9–3. A3 for Shock Trauma ICU medications.

TARGET CONDITION

Title: Shock Trauma ICU Medications

TO	John
BY	Alex
DATE	February 12, 2007

Pharmacy fills orders one by one, as they are received

Shock Trauma Rounds

E-MAIL

Pharmacy

Patients receive medication sooner

Less risk of med error

Shock Trauma ICU

No ward clerk time spent on med orders

COUNTERMEASURES

1. Use a laptop during Shock Trauma rounds to enter medication orders and send them to the pharmacy as they are completed.

IMPLEMENTATION PLAN

What	Who	When	Outcome
Acquire laptop with all necessary functions	Pete	Feb. 20	Laptop ready to be used in rounds
Inform staff of new way to order meds	Alex	Feb. 22	Staff aware of new policy
Clarify process with pharmacy	Alex	Feb. 24	New process clearly defined

COST/BENEFIT

Cost	$$$
Laptop	$1,200
Benefit	$$$
Ward clerk time saved: 728 hrs/year	$20,000
Patients receive medication sooner	Quality patient care

TEST

Borrow a laptop from IT for a 2-week trial period.
Time from order to delivery of medications significantly improved after 2-week trial.

FOLLOW UP

May 15, 2007
Medication delivery turnaround from 2-4 hours to 15-30 minutes
Workload leveled in the pharmacy (no batching) = faster medication turnaround
Medications ordered directly from rounds meeting room
More productive rounding time

CASE STUDY 3: ORTHOPEDIC DISCHARGE ROUNDING

This A3 was created in a meeting and was the genesis of the thinking and document in Appendix H, "Guidelines for Conducting a Lean Meeting." It demonstrates the use of the A3 process in a group event and highlights the importance of involving the people who can effect the change.

The authors of this book were invited to attend a meeting scheduled to address the problems associated with discharge planning for patients on a large and busy Orthopedic floor. There were three meetings already planned to tackle the issue and in conversation with the quality improvement specialist who made the invitation, this was an annual event. Every year the large team convened with best intentions of improving the process once and for all, but still all the members voiced disappointment and exasperation.

As the meeting was brought to order, it was recommended to use A3 *thinking* to establish how the work was currently happening. The meeting leader addressed the group and another member drew behind her on the whiteboard. The input of each member of the meeting was included.

The current process included a sit-down meeting of as many as 18 people every Monday and Thursday afternoon. In addition to the nursing manager and at least one bedside nurse from the floor, a dietitian, physical therapist, occupational therapist, chaplain, social worker, the three discharge coordinators, diabetic resource team member, and pharmacist attempted to attend each meeting. Additionally, the trauma coordinator, hospitalist, and other special needs department representatives attended, if they had a patient on the floor. They made sit-down "rounds" on every patient on the floor to anticipate when patients might leave the hospital and what preparations could be made to best facilitate their care after discharge.

The team voiced extreme displeasure with the system, and once the current condition was sketched and everyone agreed that it was accurate, the meeting leader queried each member, in order, around the room about his or her problems with the way work currently occurred. Every one was required to participate in identifying the issues and these were drawn on the current condition graphic as *storm clouds*.

The whiteboard barely held all of the issues, some of which included:

- Some patients arrived on Tuesday and left on Wednesday; no discharge planning occurred.

- All members sat through the whole review, when only three or four patient plans required their input.

- The discharge plan for all patients was completed on a paper form that resided on a clipboard and "floated" around the nursing station.

- Sometimes a member of the team couldn't attend, and discharge plans were incomplete.

- Physician confidence in, and use of, the discharge plan was low, since the plan was sometimes incomplete or unavailable when needed.

As the team visualized and discussed the current condition, one bright worker asked, "Why do we do this on paper anyway when we use electronic charting?" A general murmur of consent traveled around the room, and a number of people suggested ways the process should be done electronically. At this point, the meeting leader asked the group, "Who's missing in this brainstorm?" and it was recognized that they needed someone from the information technology department who understood the program to tell them what was possible. A quick phone call to the IT department brought the operative person to the meeting. Although the staff members were clear that they wanted this process to be part of an electronic record, without that key player they had no idea how or if it was possible.

The programmer not only agreed that it was a good idea, but suggested that each department define which bits of information needed to be on the discharge plan for its particular area of work. He could flex the system to pull that information from the general charting and populate a new screen, The Discharge Plan. A target condition was born and continued to grow.

Further discussion resulted in the suggestion that relevant fields of information be highlighted in a different color or font, as a reminder to the busy staff person to fill in the data required for the discharge plan. The team members believed that if they could create the plan this way, the following features (*fluffy clouds*) would exist:

- All patients would get a discharge plan, no matter the length or day of the week of their stay.

- No redundant charting would occur; caregiver or therapist would chart one time only.

- Many people could access the discharge plan for review at once.

- There would be no misplaced or unavailable discharge plans.

- MD use would be reliable.

- And the big one for the staff, NO MORE DISCHARGE PLAN- NING MEETINGS ON MONDAY AND THURSDAY!

To make the plan work, a specific implementation plan was developed to ensure that every member was assigned a date by which to create the list of information for the programmer, within a time frame that accommodated the programmer's busy schedule. While everyone wanted this work completed immediately, it was agreed to have the physical therapist create his list and work with the program- mer to test the process. The group agreed to meet in 2 weeks and review the collective information and results of the trial with the physical therapist.

At the subsequent meeting, the submissions were reviewed and the final discharge plan was formatted—one more informative than the original paper version. The work that the programmer did with the therapist was demonstrated in simulation on a laptop in the room, and the group was instantly rewarded with the results. A schedule for incorporating each department's information was com- pleted, and a target date for going live was set.

While it took a few weeks to fit this work into the IT staffer's workload, it was accomplished and tested successfully, first in simula- tion, and then live on the Orthopedic floor. The old clipboard, with directions for accessing the new electronic version, was kept for 6 months. MDs and other staff were educated at staff meetings, and bright pink notes referring to the new practice were posted beside the phones in all the doctors' dictation rooms.

Once follow-up evaluation information had been gathered and after the process was routine on the Ortho floor, other floors adopted the practice as well.

There's no way to measure the total improvement to the care of the patients after discharge or to monitor the wasted time and frus- tration experienced by the caregivers. The cost of the semi-weekly meetings for one year, however, was calculated at a whopping

$80,000. While these actual dollars will not be deducted from the bottom line, the increased worker capacity is easy to calculate from the monetary figure.

MUDAS (sources of waste): Confusion, Waiting, Defects, Processing

Relationship to the 4 RULES IN USE:

- **Rule 1: Clearly Specified Work** (*No system for electronic Discharge Plan.*)

- **Rule 2: Connections** (*Communication of information between workers not simple and direct.*)

- **Rule 3: Pathway** (*Old process for developing plan involved too many steps and people.*) See Figure 9-4.

ISSUE   *Not all patients receive complete discharge planning.*

BACKGROUND

Discharge planning is done in meetings with staff from all necessary departments on Mondays and Thursdays. 14 people attend the meetings, with an average wage of $55/hour. Meetings are an average of 1.5 hours long. 14 x $55 x 2 x 52 weeks = $80,080/year spent on discharge planning meetings.

CURRENT CONDITION

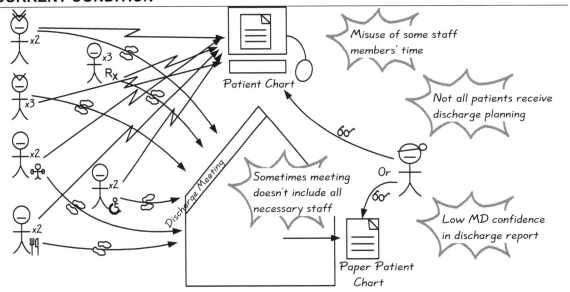

PROBLEM ANALYSIS

1. *Sometimes discharge meeting doesn't include all necessary staff.*
      Why? Attendees of meetings are not always the ones who have been treating the patient.
         Why? Representatives are sent from each department.
            Why? Staff from the department are at work and not available at the same time.
2. *Not all patients receive discharge planning.*
      Why? Some patients check in and check out before they receive it.
         Why? Discharge rounding is only done on Mondays and Thursdays.
            Why? Staff can't be taken away from work every day.
3. *Meeting is a misuse of some staff members' time.*
      Why? Staff members have to sit through the review of patients that they have not treated.
         Why? Not all patients receive care from all departments present at the meeting.
            Why? It is not always necessary.
4. *There is low MD confidence in the discharge report.*
      Why? Discharge report is sometimes incomplete.
         Why? The discharge report was not created by all the people who cared for the patient.
            Why? Not all the staff was present at the discharge meeting.
               Why? All the staff is not available to attend meetings.
                  Why? It would take too many people away from direct patient care.

Figure 9–4. A3 for orthopedic discharge rounding.

TARGET CONDITION

Title: Orthopedic Discharge Rounding

TO	Bob Johnson
BY	Elizabeth Smith
DATE	June 12, 2007

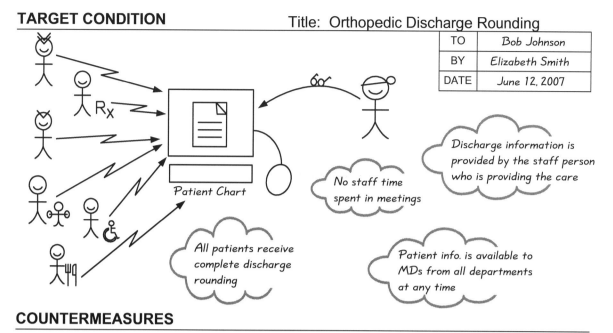

Patient Chart

No staff time spent in meetings

Discharge information is provided by the staff person who is providing the care

All patients receive complete discharge rounding

Patient info. is available to MDs from all departments at any time

COUNTERMEASURES

1. Create a discharge screen in electronic chart notes for all departments and MDs to access.
2. Educate staff on new discharge rounding process.

IMPLEMENTATION PLAN

What	Who	When	Outcome
Meet with staff to determine what info is necessary on discharge screen	Elizabeth	June 15	Discharge rounding screen criteria created
Meet with IT staff to create new discharge screen	Elizabeth	June 20	Comprehensive screen completed and online
Orient Staff	Elizabeth /IT	June 30	All staff understands new process and can use the new screen.

COST/BENEFIT

Cost	$$$
In-house development of discharge rounding screens	12 hours x $50 = $600
Benefit	$$$
Staff time saved from meeting elimination	$80,080
All patients receive accurate and timely discharge planning	Improved patient care

TEST

Each department uses the new screen in test mode for one week. Staff reviews discharge page and evaluates it for accuracy and quality of patient's discharge plan.

FOLLOW UP

New discharge planning screen has been used successfully for 6 months with the orthopedic staff. Three changes incorporated and tested. The same discharge rounding system will be implemented hospital-wide over the next 2 months.

CASE STUDY 4: HOT FOOD IN REHAB UNIT

This A3 was initiated by the nurse director of a prestigious rehabilitation unit in a regional hospital. She was concerned because the patient satisfaction scores for all areas of service in her area were historically in the high 90th percentiles with the exception of the category of "hot meals." Patient surveys scores in this section had been consistently in the mid-70s for several weeks.

Her first observation was made with a thermometer! The director of food services agreed to join her in unveiling the problem, and they checked the temperature of the hot foods and found they were at the normal serving standard. When they checked the coffee as it was poured by the kitchen workers into thermal cups, it measured at 160 degrees, not their recommended brew standard 185 degrees. It was interesting that while the rest of the hot elements of the meal were fine, because *one* item on the tray was cool, patients perceived it as a "cold tray." The change in temperature was not discernible to the touch of the people pouring, but 25 degrees had been lost by a faulty thermostat on the coffee maker. This was an easy mechanical fix, and it encouraged the staff to identify what else could be done in the process of delivering hot food.

When the entire process was followed a second time, an issue was recognized associated with the temperature-controlled transport cart, which delivered the trays from the kitchen to the nursing unit. It was a large cart, and the rehab patient care area demanded only one-third of its capacity for meal delivery. Consequently another nursing unit's trays were loaded on the same cart. The food trays for that unit were delivered first and then the cart was moved to the rehab area. Although the effect of the delay was somewhat mitigated by the temperature-controlled cart, a loss of temperature associated with the transport time ensued in all foods. This posed an expensive problem; the obvious fix was to purchase smaller temperature-controlled transport carts to service each unit individually. However, the hospital had only recently purchased the costly large carts, and the idea of replacing them wasn't feasible. The improvement team acknowledged that replacement or trade-in should be considered down the line but chose to look first at options for improving other steps in the process that would be less expensive.

The team recognized that, as the trays were being assembled, the coffee cups were filled first and assembled in horizontal rows. Often the first cup filled was the last cup used in the composition of the trays. When the food service workers discussed this dilemma, they decided to fill the cups one-by-one at the end of assembly, as the hot tray was being loaded into the temperature-controlled transport cart. This seemed reasonable to all staff present, and they agreed to try it with a simulated tray. The improvement was significant, and they agreed to test the process on the next meal and reevaluate. This created a quick fix at no cost that could be tested immediately. It was devised and approved by the people doing the work and carried a high likelihood of success. This simple process change required only brief orientation and no formal training. This change exemplifies how harnessing the knowledge and experience of the people doing the work creates a solution that is fast, friendly, and free.

The nurses and aides who delivered the trays to the patients in the unit, as well as the occupational therapist who worked with the rehab patients, were also involved when the observation team reached the nursing unit. There, they recognized that sometimes the patients weren't prepared to receive their trays, which furthered the delay of meals. Clinical staff performed a separate and effective A3 to resolve this problem.

The hospital was using a "real-time" electronic, patient-satisfaction recording tool, which allowed them to monitor the scores daily, and they saw the numbers improve immediately. When the follow-up was recorded at weeks 1, 2, and 4, the scores were consistently in the high 90s.

A couple of significant points can be made here. When the rehab director chose to delve into this problem, because it was a process problem and not a specific behavioral issue that only involved her department, the effects of her work were seen hospital wide. Because the workers involved fixed the root cause of the cold coffee problem for rehab, it improved the service to patients who drank coffee across the institution. Also, because the improvement was simple and transparent, the staff could easily amend the change if they recognized an even better way to do the work as time passed.

MUDAS (sources of waste): Defects, Motion, Waiting

Relationship to the 4 RULES IN USE:

- **Rule 3: Pathways.** (*Unnecessary steps prevented food service workers from delivering a cup of hot coffee from the coffee maker to the patient.*) See Figure 9–5.

ISSUE *Patients complain that meals are not hot in the Rehab Unit.*

BACKGROUND

Patient satisfaction survey results are less than 80% for hot meals. Meals are on large carts and often travel to other floors before arriving at the Rehab Unit.

CURRENT CONDITION

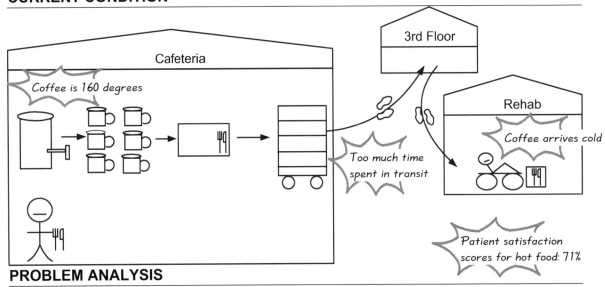

PROBLEM ANALYSIS

1. Coffee arrives cool at the patients' bedside

     Why? The coffee is not coming out of the coffee maker at the specified temperature (180 degrees)

         Why? The thermostat in the coffee maker is faulty

     Why? The coffee sits in cups for a long period of time while the trays are being assembled

         Why? Cups are poured in advance and arranged with other beverages to be added to the tray as prescribed

2. Food spends too much time in transit

     Why? Trays travel from kitchen to the 3rd floor before being delivered to Rehab

         Why? Delivery carts are large and trays for more than one unit are loaded together on one cart

         Why? Delivery carts are designed for more trays than there are patients in Rehab

Figure 9–5. A3 for hot food in rehab unit.

TARGET CONDITION

Title: Hot Food in Rehab Unit

TO	Tim
BY	Jane
DATE	March 5, 2007

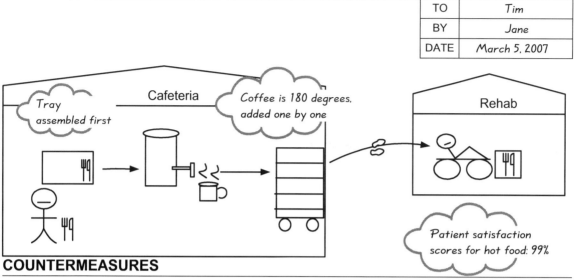

COUNTERMEASURES

1. Repair thermostat in coffee maker.
2. Rearrange order of filling coffee cups to fill one by one at the end of tray assembly.
3. Deliver trays to patients in order of assembly.

IMPLEMENTATION PLAN

What	Who	When	Outcome
Replace thermostat in coffee maker	Jane	March 12	Coffee will come out at 180 degrees
Re-order the assembly of trays so that coffee is poured and put on trays just before they leave the kitchen	Jane	March 20	Coffee will spend less time on the tray before arriving to patient
Use smaller transport carts so they carry only one unit's trays	Jane/ Tim	April 1	Less travel time from kitchen to Rehab
Educate staff re: delivering trays from top of cart to bottom to avoid 1st loaded tray spending most time on cart	Tim	April 5	Trays will all be warm when delivered

COST/BENEFIT

Cost	$$$
Thermostat for coffee maker	$8.50
Benefit	$$$
Patients are satisfied with the temperature of the food they recieve	Patient Satisfaction

FOLLOW UP

May 30, 2007 – Patient satisfaction scores for hot food: 100%

CASE STUDY 5: RECOVERY ROOM TIME

This busy A3 was done at the request of an orthopedic surgeon who felt that he could complete five total joint procedures a day but was being limited to four a day by a bottleneck in the Post Anesthesia Care Unit (recovery room). The surgeon was frustrated because he had a waitlist of patients that extended care for 6 weeks. Because his patients received spinal anesthesia, he anticipated that they should be fully awake within 30 to 40 minutes. His personal investigation confirmed they spent an average of 95 minutes in the recovery room. Nursing ratio to patient in this critical area was 1:1.

The improvement team observed the recovery of one of the surgeon's patients, and the current condition drawing was created. The patient was in the recovery area almost 90 minutes. The team kept track of the activities performed by the hardworking and capable nurse. They noticed four major things as they observed and drew.

The first activity that appeared flawed was obtaining and validating the post-operative X-ray. After the technician took the portable X-ray, he left the recovery room to process the film. On his return he took the film out of the envelope and hung it on the X-ray view box, across the department from the patient's bed. The nurse asked her coworker to watch her patient and took the X-ray off the view box, put it back in the envelope, and left the department to find the surgeon to approve the film. When the sketch was shown to both the radiology technician and the nurse for validation, they looked at each other and asked the same question. *Why doesn't the tech take the film to the doctor for approval?* The staff had been working this way for so long that they didn't stop to consider another way, but the illustration made the waste clear. On the spot they agreed to try out the suggestion on the *next patient*. The tech would not come into the recovery area and hang the film, but go straight to the surgeon. The X-ray could then be returned to the radiology department directly, which eliminated the annoying hassles that occurred when a film was misplaced. It was such an easy fix that it didn't need approval from a superior and was immediately successful. This step alone increased the RN's time with the patient by 6 minutes.

The second obvious roadblock to the nurse was the location of supplies. Almost no supplies were available at the point of care, and she made 16 trips to the storage area across the busy room! This congested the area, left the patient unattended, and created disruption and frustration for the RN. Upon discussion, the nurses realized that they used the same materials for patients 90 percent of the time. In review of the current condition drawing, the affected nurses enthusiastically agreed that decentralizing the stock and making it mobile would be a huge improvement. The nurses expressed repeated concerns for leaving the bedside of their patients.

The third and fourth problems involved the telephone. The nurse was called to the telephone, located far from the patient care area, seven times. When the patient was ready to leave the PACU, the nurse called to give report to the receiving nurse on the unit. The unit clerk answered the call and attempted to find the busy floor nurse to receive the report. The recovery nurse was on hold 7 minutes, waiting to give report. While reviewing the current state A3, one recovery nurse, who had become interested in the drawing, said, *"Didn't you know? That nurse now has a cell phone that you can call directly."*

Several other interruptions and an amazing amount of duplicate charting were noted, but only the problems above were addressed on this A3. The breakdown of the 90 minutes spent on busy activities with the patient revealed some staggering numbers:

- 33 minutes doing paperwork
- 29 minutes on the telephone, clarifying orders, giving report, or on hold
- 6 minutes out of the room
- 9 minutes finding supplies
- 13 minutes actually caring for the patient

The target condition was developed with all the recovery room staff, and they were eager to get the new method in motion.

The test from the first problem was conducted with the next patient and six minutes of patient caretime was captured. The nurse manager agreed to obtain a rolling cart, on which staff would load the supplies for two patients at a time and park between those two patients' beds. With two trials, the staff finally approved a set of hand-carry totes. The nurses would gather supplies before the patient arrived and keep them at the bedside. Unused stock could be returned to the shelves at the end of the day.

The telephone issue required some capital expenditure and took 2 weeks to implement. The hospital purchased cordless extensions of the main phone and placed them strategically in the patient care areas for convenience, and programmed updated commonly dialed numbers into the speed dial function.

Three weeks after the initial observation, the improvement team observed the recovery care for four patients of the same surgeon. These patients had undergone joint replacement surgery that day.

The average recovery room time for those patients was 63 minutes. While this was still in excess of what the physician thought was ideal, 108 minutes of recovery nurse time was captured, more than enough time to accommodate another joint replacement patient.

Consider the improvement for all of the stakeholders. The surgeon, anesthesiologist, and hospital gain the revenue of another case done per day. The patient's bill is less for the expensive recovery room time, and the patient waitlist is reduced by 20 percent.

MUDAS (Source of Waste): Confusion, Motion, Waiting, Defects

Relationship to the 4 RULES IN USE:

- **Rule 2: Connections.** (*There was not a direct connection between the recovery room nurse and the receiving nurse.*)
- **Rule 3: Pathways.** (*Nurses needed to make many trips to the supply room and the telephone.*)

(*The nurse's travel between the X-ray view box and the doctor was not essential.*)

For a comprehensive view of the A3 document, see Figure 9–6.

ISSUE *Only four total joint (TJR) replacement patients can receive surgery per day.*

BACKGROUND

The surgeon believes he could perform five operations on Monday, but the bottleneck in the recovery room limits the capacity to four. Surgeon states his patients need 30–40 minutes of recovery time, but the patients are spending an average of 90 minutes in the recovery room.

CURRENT CONDITION

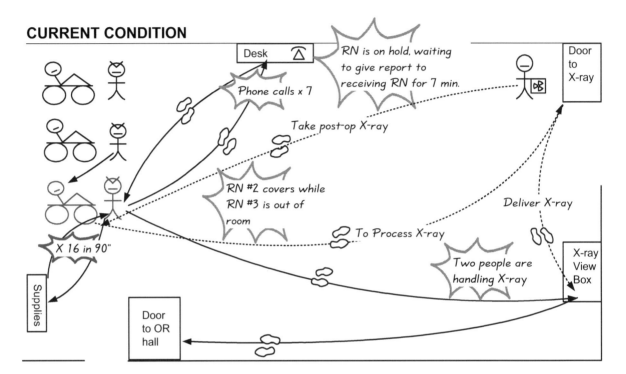

PROBLEM ANALYSIS

1. *RN #2 covers RN #3's patient while she is out of the room*
    Why? RN #3 has to use the phone at the desk call the receiving RN to give report
        Why? There are no phones available at the point of care
    Why? RN #3 spends time on hold while calling the receiving RN
        Why? RN #3 has to call the ward clerk and wait for receiving RN to answer
            Why? RN #3 doesn't have a direct phone number to the receiving RN
    Why? RN travels out of recovery room to deliver X-ray to MD

2. *The RN makes many trips to the supply room*
    Why? All necessary supplies are stored away from patient bedside
        Why? Location of storage shelves

Figure 9–6. A3 for recovery room time.

TARGET CONDITION

Title: Recovery Room Time

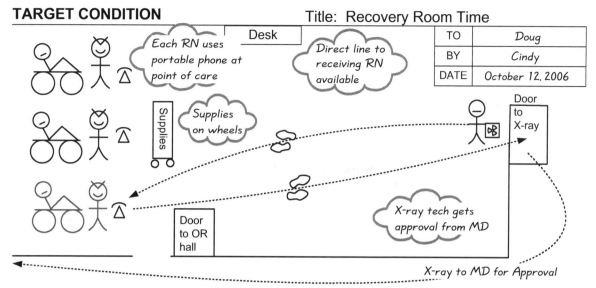

TO	Doug
BY	Cindy
DATE	October 12, 2006

COUNTERMEASURES

1. Radiology tech takes the X-ray to the MD for approval.
2. Use cordless extension phones (one between two patients) with speed dial codes for the comfort zone and X-ray.
3. Make patient supplies portable.

IMPLEMENTATION PLAN

What	Who	When	Outcome
Educate radiology techs re: taking X-rays directly to MD	Jason	10/13/06	New process implemented
Purchase cordless extensions of main phone	Cindy	10/20/06	Phones available at patient bedside
Collect and program speed dial numbers for essential contacts	Cindy	10/20/06	Phones and speed dial ready to use
Obtain cart for portable supply system	Cindy	11/1/06	Patient supplies available at bedside

COST/BENEFIT

Cost	$$$
Cordless phones, cart	$389
Benefit	$$$
One more TJR / day = 20% less delay to surgery for patient	20% more income
Reduce patient bill and increase RN-to-patient time	Quality

TEST

Borrow cart and stock point of care supplies
Use cell phones for trial x 1 week
Note RN time saved from not leaving the patients bedside

FOLLOW UP

November 28, 2006
Average patient time in recovery room: 63 minutes
This is enough time to add another TJR patient per surgical day

CASE STUDY 6: FIBER-OPTIC ENDOSCOPE REPAIRS

This A3 was authored by an anesthesiologist (his first A3, done in a reVIEW© Course,[1] supported by a coach) concerned and frustrated by the alarming number of incidents of damaged fiber-optic endoscopes on his cart in the previous year. The damage meant that scopes were often unavailable when needed for surgical patients, and the cost of repairs and replacements for that period of time for all staff anesthesiologists was a staggering $48,400. This doctor was initially concerned with those problems only, but in the course of his observation, revealed another important, albeit subtle, safety issue.

In his initial observation of a peer using this equipment, he quickly recognized that because the expensive, flexible scope was placed on top of the anesthesia cart (used to store and access medication and other anesthesia equipment), it was easy for the end of the scope to fall into an open drawer. As the drawer was closed (usually hastily) the scope could be caught in the closure and damaged.

Secondly, it was observed that no documented proof indicated whether or not the scope had been used as the procedure progressed and the changeover staff arrived to clean the room. In most cases a single anesthesiologist used the scope, but occasionally a transfer of staff occurred during a lengthy procedure, and a used tube could be recycled as clean, creating a contamination risk.

In his observation, the anesthesiologist questioned the observed doctor, a circulating nurse, and the changeover crew to validate what he had seen and what he knew from his own experience. Staff also volunteered additional stories of other near misses.

In this case, the author of the A3 was the director of surgery. When he established consensus from the other staff involved that his proposed *target condition* sounded like a sensible alternative to the way they currently worked, he proceeded to the test, which was to try his proposal on his own anesthesia cart for 2 weeks. He agreed to report back to them at that time with his personal experience.

The person doing the work (the anesthesiologist) recognized a personal source of frustration, observed a peer with the same frustra-

---

1. reVIEW® (realizing exceptional Value In Everyday Work) Course. Education/implementation program taught by Lean Healthcare West and authored by Cindy Jimmerson.

tion, and discovered not only the root cause of the focused problem but a potential for patient contagion. The simple and inexpensive solution of storage chambers made from PVC pipe on each cart made the fix quick, inexpensive, and easy to test and monitor. The test was concluded in 2 days instead of 2 weeks, and the other anesthesiologists requested identical modifications of their carts. Also noted in the test was an unanticipated problem with cleaning the "dirty" tubes, and a second A3 was quickly done with the cleaning staff to devise a way to ensure that contaminated scopes and storage tubes were not overlooked in the room changeover. The *follow-up* documentation at 6 months confirmed that the safely stored scopes were less likely to be damaged, and actually reported zero damages from the storage source.

MUDAS (Sources of Waste): Confusion, Motion, Delay, Defects

ROOT CAUSES:

- There was no specified safe storage for fiber-optic endoscopes on the anesthesia cart during surgery.

- *Clean* and *used* fiber-optic endoscopes were not easy to differentiate.

COUNTERMEASURES:

- Create a clearly marked location on all anesthesia carts for fiber-optic endoscopes.

- Indicate on each tube "Clean" and "Used."

Relationship to the 4 RULES IN USE

- **Rule 1: Activities of work clearly specified**. (*There was no specified safe storage for fiber-optic endoscopes on the anesthesia cart during surgery*.) See Figure 9-7.

ISSUE *Fiber-optic Endoscopes (FEs) are unavailable when needed because they are frequently broken or being repaired.*

BACKGROUND

From June 2003–June 2004, $48,400 was spent repairing and replacing FEs

CURRENT CONDITION

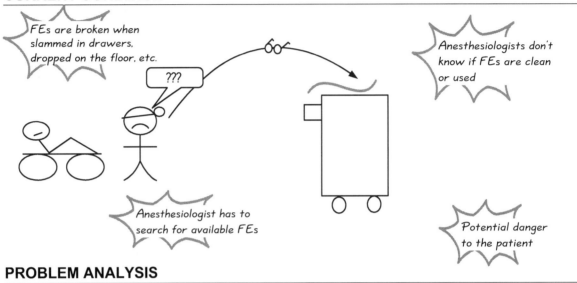

FEs are broken when slammed in drawers, dropped on the floor, etc.

Anesthesiologists don't know if FEs are clean or used

???

Anesthesiologist has to search for available FEs

Potential danger to the patient

PROBLEM ANALYSIS

1. Anesthesiologists waste time searching for fiber-optic endoscopes
    Why? FEs are not always available
        Why? FEs are broken when slammed in drawers, dropped on the floor, etc.
            Why? They are placed on top of the anesthesia cart before and after surgery
                Why? There is no secure location to put them on the anesthesia cart
2. There is potential danger to the patients' health
    Why? There is confusion over whether or not FEs are clean or used
        Why? There is no designated location for clean FEs and used FEs on the anesthesia cart

Figure 9–7. A3 for fiber-optic endoscope repairs.

TARGET CONDITION

Title: Fiber-optic Endoscope Repairs

TO	Mark
BY	Joe
DATE	10 July, 2007

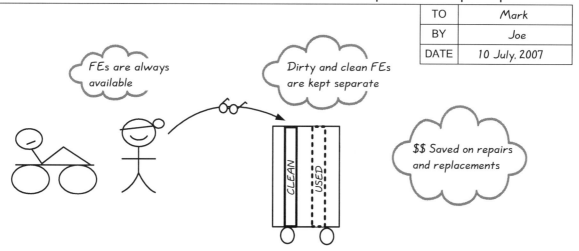

COUNTERMEASURES

1. Put two tubes (PVC pipe) on the anesthesiologists' cart for FEs. Designate one tube for clean FEs and one for dirty FEs.
2. Contact sterile processing about tubes on the carts.

IMPLEMENTATION PLAN

What	Who	When	Outcome
Buy supplies for anesthesia cart tubes	Joe	July 15	All supplies available
Put tubes on cart and label "Clean" and "Used"	Joe	July 18	Tubes ready for use
Talk to sterile processing and OR staff	Joe	July 22	Sterile processing aware of new system

COST/BENEFIT

Cost	$$$
PVC Pipe	$5.50
Hardwear	$4.10
Total Cost	$9.60
Benefit	$$$
No repair/replacement of FE	$48,400
Increase patient safety	Quality and Compliance

TEST

One anesthesiologist will retrofit cart with inexpensive, marked tubing X two weeks, and report back.

FOLLOW UP

February 1, 2007 – Anesthesiologists have been using this system for six months, and have had no broken FE's

CASE STUDY 7: MEDICARE CLAIMS DENIALS

The investigator in this case study was trying to determine the source of medical claims for which payment was denied by Medicare. His interest in this problem was raised by the CFO, who was alarmed at the sum of money which did not come to the hospital on the first request.

When the investigator went to the billing department and collected *denials* information from the previous fiscal quarter, he was surprised to find that 42 percent of those denied claims were the results of "names not matching." As he observed the process of the billing department constructing the bill, he discovered that the name that appeared on the bill was collected at the time of admission by the admitting department.

Observation of the process in the admitting department revealed that sometimes the admitting agent only asked the patient his name and did not actually see the patient's Medicare ID card. The patient sometimes used a name other than his legal name (for example, James Smith vs. Richard James Smith) or used a shortened version (Fred vs. Frederick).

To the further confusion of the admissions staff, the public relations department had encouraged them to make the admission process as easy for patients as possible and they felt asking for the card was violating the hospital policy of kindness.

Admissions submitted the demographic information to a central database, therefore the wrong identifier traveled with the patient throughout his or her stay. This occurred, not only when charges were incurred in the clinical areas, but also when the bill dropped after discharge and coding. Hence the bill sent to Medicare could easily be submitted with a name that did not match the name of the patient registered with Medicare, resulting in a denial of payment.

When the denial was received (instead of payment), the billing office staff would begin the rework of determining the patient's correct billing name and confirming that charges for the patient were correct. Because of the confusion created by two names on the record, it was easy to miss charges or add incorrect charges from another patient with a similar name. It was discovered that some patients had three or more medical record numbers because of the name confusion.

This seemingly simple issue had been recurring for as long as anyone could remember, because the responsibility for creating the bill resided in the billing department. No one looked at where the problem resided in the process until the investigator started asking *why* the names didn't match; no one went to the front office where the patient entered the system to fix the problem. This example demonstrates the value of fixing problems as far *upstream* in a process as possible to get to the root cause and maximize the results of improvement efforts.

As with most A3s, once the investigation of this issue began, other associated problems were identified. Several changes to the process improved the accuracy of the bill, as well as reducing redundant work and improving cash flow.

MUDAS (sources of waste): Confusion, Waiting, Overproduction, Defects

ROOT CAUSE: The admission process was undefined and most registrars hadn't included verifying the name on the Medicare card.

COUNTERMEASURES:

- Clearly specify the activities of the admission process.
- Convert old charts with multiple names to one legal name.

Relationship to the 4 RULES IN USE

- **Rule 1: Specify the work.** (*Not all admission staff used the same method of identifying patients. Medicare cards were intermittently validated. Admission staff was never made aware that names did not match.*)

For a comprehensive look at this A3 process, consult Figure 9–8.

ISSUE *Patients' medical claims are being denied by Medicare.*

BACKGROUND / MEASUREMENT

In the previous year, $1.17 million in delayed Medicare payments. 42% of Medicare denials resulted from the patient's name on the medical claim not matching the patient's name with the insurance company = $491,400/year.

CURRENT CONDITION

PROBLEM ANALYSIS

1. *Payment is not received for medical claims from Medicare*
   Why? Medicare denies payment
   Why? The name on the medical claim doesn't match the registered Medicare name
   Why? Patient's common name is entered into the hospital computer
   Why? Admissions doesn't always verify the patient's insurance card
   Why? Patient services department encourages Admissions staff to make things as easy for patients as possible
   Why? Admission activity is not clearly specified

2. *Incorrect charges to patients*
   Why? The charges of another patient with a similar name may be captured incorrectly
   Why? Confusion when more than one name is used for the patient
   Why? Patient is not admitted with registered Medicare name
   Why? Admissions doesn't always ask for the patient's insurance card
   Why? Patient services department encourages Admissions staff to make things as easy for patients as possible
   Why? Admission activity is not clearly specified

Figure 9–8. A3 for Medicare claims denials.

TARGET CONDITION

Title: Medicare Claims Denials

TO	Jane
BY	Bob
DATE	April 15, 2006

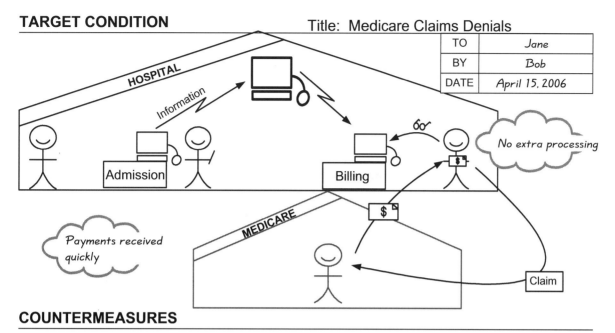

COUNTERMEASURES

1. Clearly specify the activities of the admission process to include verifying name on Medicare card.
2. Convert old charts with multiple names to one legal name.

IMPLEMENTATION PLAN

What	Who	When	Outcome
Define best admission process	Managers & Staff, Billing & Admission	May 1, 2003	Admission process defined
Create visual guides for the new process. Laminate & post in work area.	Manager	May 2, 2003	Clear signal for staff. No reliance on staff memory.
Collate multiple accounts of each patient into one account	Medical records staff	By 8/1/03	One reference account per patient

COST/BENEFIT

Cost	$$$
Staff time to define process (7 staff X 5 hours)	35 hours
Benefit	$$$
Accurate charges on patient bill, accurate medical records	Quality
Reduced accounts receivable days	Improved cash flow

TEST

Try new process X one week and review for revisions

FOLLOW UP

November 1, 2006
Total delayed Medicare payments for the last 6 months = $263,860
Delayed Medicare payments from names not matching from last 6 months = $14,100

CASE STUDY 8: MEDICAL SURGICAL STOCKROOMS

The following A3 is one of several that evolved from a specific incident in which a nurse couldn't find unique dressing material prescribed for a post-operative patient. As the nurse's search was documented in the current condition, it became apparent that the location and labeling of inventory on the floor was problematic. Other issues were recognized related to the delay in the patient receiving her fresh dressing, and this A3 dealt only with the inventory problem. Together with the other A3s completed around the incident, a much-improved process was created for providing clinical materials close at hand.

This A3 ultimately improved the placement of materials on the unit to match the areas of most frequent work. By understanding what was being used, by whom, and in the most frequent locations, the improvement team actually reduced the amount of stock on the floor, as well as the number of "stock-out" calls to Materials Management (MM). These were the measurable improvements. The "soft," but equally important changes resulted in nurse availability time gained, and delay of care to the patient decreased.

The issue was brought to a monthly meeting of Medical/Surgical (M/S) charge nurses. It had been a longstanding source of frustration for nurses and MM.

The physical layout of the long ward with the nursing station and medication preparation room in the middle created a hub of movement and activity near the center. See Figure 9–9.

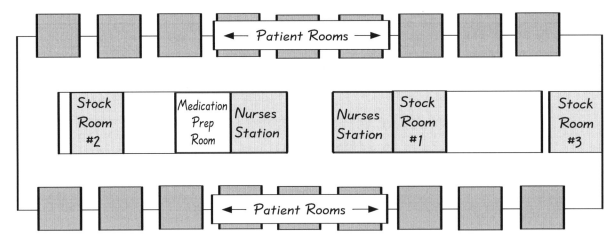

Figure 9–9. Map shows layout of busy Medical/Surgical hub.

The stockroom nearest the center was the most frequently used and quickest to be depleted. The other two storerooms lie further from the nurse's desk; one had similar, but not exactly the same inventory, and the third held a locked, catch-all of random equipment. Labeling in rooms 1 and 2 was done on bins for small items and shelves for larger materials; the small, black-and-white, difficult-to-read font was not always accurate. Stockroom 3 was unlabeled but often housed valuable equipment. The Materials

116

Management department was responsible for arrangement, stocking, and labeling of stockrooms 1 and 2. The staff from that department labeled materials using the name on their inventory record, not always the common name used by the clinical staff. When interviewed, no one claimed responsibility for stockroom 3. The nurses would often call MM to request an article that was already on the unit—its location labeled with an unfamiliar name.

Over time, the nurses lost faith in an article being available in either storeroom 2 or 3 (the rooms most distant from the nurse's station). If the shelves of storeroom 1 didn't contain the sought-after item, they would commonly forego the long walk to the other storage rooms, or in lieu of a questionable search, would request delivery of the item from MM while sometimes it was already in the unit inventory and somewhere on the floor. Overall, evidence in a single day's observation clearly validated that the process was sorely broken. The activities of *stocking the unit* (by MM) and *using the supplies* (by patient care staff) occurred in silos; communication between the two departments was rare outside of complaints.

The improvement team included one charge nurse from the M/S unit, the MM worker responsible for restocking the rooms, a staff nurse, and a patient care aide. After independent observations, they met to develop the left side of the A3 and took it to their peers for validation. Minor additions were made and enthusiasm for fixing this chronically annoying problem grew.

The team met with a number of the M/S staff, drew a target condition sketch on a whiteboard in the unit break room, and included the input of several nurses and aides as they passed in and out. This didn't require a meeting to garner enough information to create a reasonable plan for a more efficient way to work.

By listening to both clinical staff (MDs and nurses) and the ancillary workers who did much of the routine bedside care (patient care aides), the improvement team was able to identify patterns of use for materials in specific storerooms. File data compiled by MM was reviewed to determine daily usage. (They had been collecting data for years on the rate of use but had never used that information.)

The team discovered that the distant storerooms were used mostly by the aides, who did routine care using daily personal items (basins/urinals, etc.), for which there was no charge and that the charged items for medication delivery and dressing changes were not often used in those areas. Everyone got involved with weeding out obsolete and infrequently used items, resulting in frequent hilarity as some stock was deemed unrecognizable or unused for many years!

As an illustration of the changes they made in stock, consider the use and rearrangement of *one* item in Figures 9–10 and 9–11.

This commonly used item was chosen to test the new distribution plan (for 3 days at high census) and the results are listed in Figure 9–12.

Current Condition:

	Stockroom 1	Stockroom 2	Stockroom 3
Stocked	**9**	**9**	**9**
Used	**13**	**1**	**0**

Stock out calls to Materials Management for this item: **4**

Figure 9–10. Some stockrooms contain too much of one particular item, whereas another room does not store enough.

Target Condition:

	Stockroom 1	Stockroom 2	Stockroom 3
Stocked	**15**	**2**	**1**

Reduction in overall stock of this item on the unit: **9**

Figure 9–11. The target condition better reflects the department's actual needs.

Test Results:

	Stockroom 1	Stockroom 2	Stockroom 3
Stocked	**15**	**2**	**1**
Used	**14**	**0**	**0**

Stock out calls to Materials Management for this item: **0**

Reduction in overall stock of this item on the unit: **13**

Figure 9–12. Follow-up after 3 months.

The test results revealed some interesting things. The first was that the close look at usage in each stockroom was key to stocking the right amount of an item in the most appropriate locations. The staff members also acknowledged that because they were all involved in developing and validating the target condition, they saw the value of centralizing the clinical materials to the nurses' work area, and they stopped looking in the distant rooms. This in itself reduced staff travel tremendously. After this process was followed up and honed over several months, the unneeded items in Figures 10 through 12 were removed from storerooms 2 and 3, further reducing unnecessary inventory.

The ancillary staff members also recognized that the items they used most were handier in stockrooms 2 and 3 and requested that larger items be moved from stockroom 1 to make space for the clinical equipment and concentrate their gear where they knew they would have a consistent supply. Everyone agreed that a simple easy-to-read inventory list in each room would save miles of travel and eliminate reliance on memory.

Two other significant improvements resulted from this A3, each completed on a separate A3 form:

1. A dressing cart was designed by the staff to make disposable charge items for dressing changes mobile. It went through several iterations before it was perfected but was ultimately successful.

2. Materials Management recognized that some less frequently used dressing materials would be better requested one by one, and this resulted in additional reduction of materials on the floor that took up space and didn't turn over quickly. Those *special order* items were also listed on the inventory list in the stockrooms to alleviate confusion.

Ultimately this activity resulted in a $7,800+ reduction of residing stock on the floor and a decline of stock-out calls to MM per week from 39 to 4. While the evaluation of interruptions is difficult to compute, the obvious improvement of workflow in both departments was appreciable.

More difficult to measure, but quite obvious and no less important, was the reduction in delay of care to the patient and frustration and wasted time of the nursing staff. With a constant eye on concern for patient safety and consistent care, this inventory problem, which in the old way of thinking may have been only considered for financial reasons, was now linked to the quality of care.

For an A3 review of this case study, see Figure 9–13.

MUDAS (sources of waste): Confusion, Motion, Waiting, Processing, Inventory, Defects, Overproduction

ROOT CAUSES:

- Essential materials were not located consistently and reliably near the work.
- Materials were not always labeled correctly or easy to find.
- There was no clear indication of what inventory resided in each stockroom for the users.

COUNTERMEASURES:

- Arrange and label all materials to support the clinical work.
- Eliminate all unnecessary inventory.
- Create quick reference list of inventory to post in each room.

Relationship to the 4 RULES IN USE

- **Rule 1: Work not clearly specified.**
    (How/where do we find our supplies? [clinical unit staff])
    (Exactly what should we stock in each stockroom? [MM staff])

ISSUE *Patient's dressing change is delayed while nurse looks for unavailable supplies.*

BACKGROUND

There are three stockrooms on the MS unit. If materials aren't found in the stockrooms, materials management is called to deliver needed items. Average number of stock-out calls to materials management per week = 39.

CURRENT CONDITION

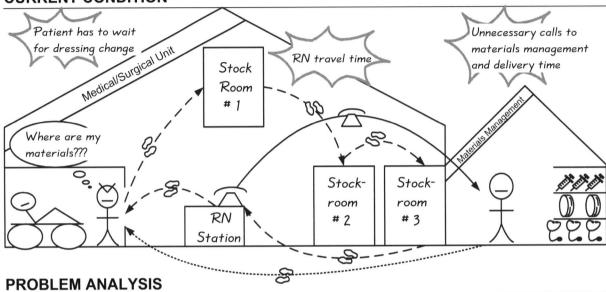

PROBLEM ANALYSIS

1. Patient has to wait for his/her dressing change
   Why? RN can't find necessary materials
     Why? Materials are not in stockrooms
       Why? Some items in stockroom depleted quicker than others
       Why? Materials are not stocked according to demand
     Why? Materials are labeled with a different name than the commonname used by staff
       Why? Materials management label and stock storeroom with inventory
   record name
         Why? MM unaware of different names used
     Why? Labels on materials are difficult to read
       Why? Materials are labeled in small black-and-white font
2. Lots of RN travel time
   Why? RN looks for supplies in three different stock rooms
     Why? No easy reference of inventory of stock rooms
3. Unnecessary RN and MM time spent on phone call and deliveries
   Why? RN can't find necessary materials
     Why? As above

Figure 9–13. A3 for Medical Surgical stockrooms.

TARGET CONDITION

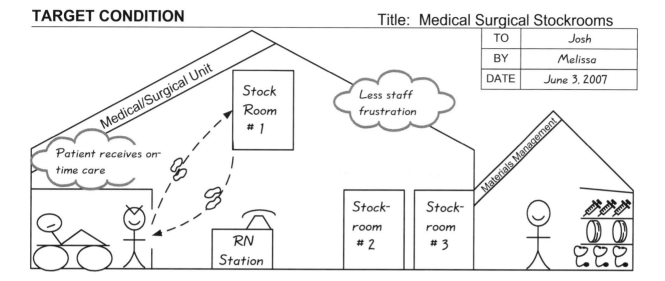

Title: Medical Surgical Stockrooms

TO	Josh
BY	Melissa
DATE	June 3, 2007

COUNTERMEASURES

1. Stock materials on the MS unit to match the demand.
2. Create quick reference list of inventory in each stockroom.

IMPLEMENTATION PLAN

What	Who	When	Outcome
Evaluate the usage of materials in the stockrooms	MS staff	6/10-30, 2005	Clear illustration of what inventory is needed & in which stockrooms
Rearrange materials in stockrooms	MS & MM	7/5/05	Materials in MS stockrooms match the need of staff on the unit
Create quick reference list of inventory	MM staff	7/15/05	Inventory list of all materials and locations in each stockroom

COST/COST BENEFIT

Cost	$$$
Materials management and RN staff time	18 hours
Benefit	$$$
Saved MS/MM staff time	1.5 hours/shift
Patient receives direct care	Quality
Unused material removed from MS inventory	$7,691

TEST

Rearrange stockroom #1 and monitor stock-out calls.

FOLLOW UP

Materials management monitors stock-out calls per week at 30 days and 120 days.
Result @ 30 days: Average stock-out calls per week - 7*
Result @ 120 days: Average stock-out calls per week - 4

*On investigation it was discovered that this was intentional. It was agreed that a large volume of dressings needed for specific patients would be ordered from MM one by one.

121

CASE STUDY 9: NICU ISOLETTE RENTAL

This case study uncovered an extended area of waste when a single concern was raised in one department with a process later shared throughout the clinical organization.

The manager of a busy newborn nursery was alarmed at the amount of the department budget spent in the recent quarter on rental equipment. When she began investigating the charges, she found that, in her department, the rental use was predominately for newborn isolettes. The number of isolette rentals exceeded what she calculated was valid for the recent census of newborns.

Rentals were requested from the vendor by the nursing staff, but the Biomed department processed the machines in and out of the hospital. The NICU manager contacted the Biomed manager, and they initiated the following A3, focusing on the recent rental of a single isolette.

The machine in question had been rented at a busy time when the hospital-owned isolette inventory was fully in use with current census, including a set of triplet newborns. When the triplets were discharged from the NICU, the three isolettes were cleaned and returned to the utility room (two hospital-owned, one rental). Another delivery occurred immediately after, and the attending nurse took one of the isolettes (the rental) to the delivery room and put it to use for the newest baby. This isolette remained in circulation, being used for several subsequent babies, while the regular hospital inventory sat in the utility room unused. Rental fees continued to accumulate as unnecessary overhead for the department. The following factors contributed to the confusion and unnecessary expense.

First, the rentals were the same brand and function as the department machines (sensible, everyone knew how to use them). However, each was marked with a faint engraving near the rear wheel, and it wasn't readily noticeable that it was a rental machine. When the nurses were queried, most acknowledged that they were unfamiliar with distinguishing between rentals and nonrentals, and assumed that Biomed took care of returning the rentals.

The Biomed staff member who participated on this A3 realized that his department had always waited for the nursing units to request the return of equipment but couldn't identify an activity that triggered the request. Even as they explored the return process for the isolettes, he started thinking of all the other rental equipment in other departments in the same pattern of *use, clean, store,* and *use again.* The potential size of this problem loomed large.

The current condition drawing and subsequent *storm clouds* of the specific isolette issue addressed in this A3 revealed a variety of problems, all of which were easy to remedy and carried significant cost implications. The greater value was realized in discovering the scope of the rental equipment management problem house-wide. This A3 spawned a series of similar A3s specific to other kinds of equipment and locations. Because of the learning gained with the first A3, each subsequent one was created with more speed and detail.

This scenario is not uncommon. When looking at the *process,* not the people, involved with a specific incident, the high-level view assumes the look of a template that suits many work situations. Making the leap from thinking in terms of a specific issue to a more global or general application is easy and always profitable. It generates more observation, communication, and *thinking* as the process moves from department to department and activity to activity, which in turn improves relationships among the workers involved in the improvement. This type of improvement quickly generates a life of its own, with workers devising more applications than anyone initially intended.

MUDAS (sources of waste): Confusion, Inventory, Overproduction

ROOT CAUSES:

- There was no clearly defined process for returning rented equipment when it was no longer needed on the unit.

- It was not easy to distinguish rental equipment from hospital-owned machines.

COUNTERMEASURES:

- The process for returning a piece of equipment was printed on the tag in a large, easy-to-read font.

- Simple, bright orange, two-part tags were attached to the rental isolettes by the Biomed department when they went to the nursing unit. (One part of the tag was retained by Biomed to keep track of rental equipment location and age).

Relationship to the 4 RULES IN USE:

- **Rule 1: Specify the work.** (*The way to return rental equipment was not defined.*)

- **Rule 2: Connections.** (*Communication between the house-keeper or nurse who cleaned the isolette and Biomed wasn't simple or direct. Many times the machine would be labeled "clean" with a sticky note or the housekeeper would pass the message to a nurse or ward clerk. Depending on the experience of the person receiving the information, that person would then do one of several different things to get the equipment returned to Biomed, usually involving another layer of reporting the status of the item.*)

- **Rule 3: Pathways.** (*Again, because there was no clearly defined process, the pathway, or steps required to return the machine to the vendor were too numerous, too complex, and involved too many people. The process of returning material was not reliable or consistent.*)

- **Rule 4: Improvement.** (*In spite of the frustration of not finding equipment when it was needed and confusion about paying rental bills, this broken "un-process" had been limping along for years. Staff had not been clear about how many isolettes the department really owned, assuming several rentals belonged to the hospital. In the design of the bright indicator tag was included a comment section for staff to send notes to Biomed. When staff members were oriented to the new tag and return procedure, they were encouraged to send comments via this method. This created a conduit for continuing to improve the use of valuable rental equipment.*)

In this case study, the design of the tag is also worth highlighting. The team used an impossible-to-miss color that anyone could identify from a distance. The tag was located out of the way of the work space but clearly visible below the bassinette area. This eliminated the easy error of confusing rental with owned machines. Also the process for returning was printed directly on the tag, where it was available at the time and point of use. The tag was attached to the machine, eliminating the possibility of a return form being lost or not traveling with the machine to Biomed. The tag also was a two-piece tag, with one piece torn off and hung on a board in the Biomed work area at the time of issue to indicate the specific department where it was in use. This allowed the number of rentals in any given department to be monitored at a glance by Biomed staff.

Although this specific change seemed small, the result was noteworthy, and the other changes, sparked by this first activity, rippled improvement through the organization. For a detailed look at the A3 from this process, see Figure 9–14.

ISSUE *The amount of money being spent in the NICU on rental equipment exceeded the demand for rental equipment.*

BACKGROUND

The NICU has 10 isolettes and the capacity of 12 newborns. The normal census is eight newborns. When the census exceeds ten newborns, NICU rents isolettes.
In 6 months $63,000 was spent on rental isolettes.

CURRENT CONDITION

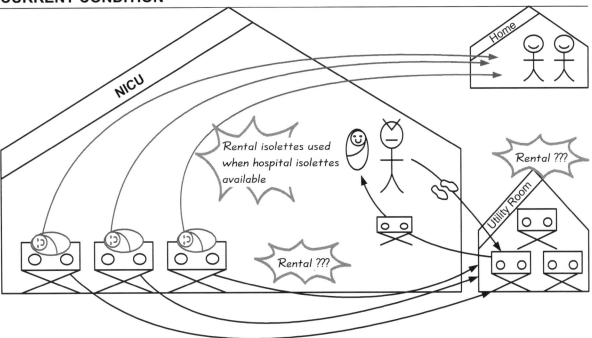

PROBLEM ANALYSIS

1. *Rental isolettes are being used when hospital isolettes are available*
    Why? Rental isolettes are stored in the utility room after use
        Why? All isolettes are the same model and look the same
            Why? Rental isolettes aren't clearly marked as rentals
2. *Rental isolettes aren't returned to Biomed after use*
    Why? RN's can't easily recognize rental vs. hospital owned isolettes
        Why? No clear identification as rental
    Why? No defined process for returning isolettes

Figure 9–14. A3 for NICU Isolette Rental.

TARGET CONDITION

Title: NICU Isolette Rental

TO	Jennifer
BY	Alex
DATE	April 1, 2007

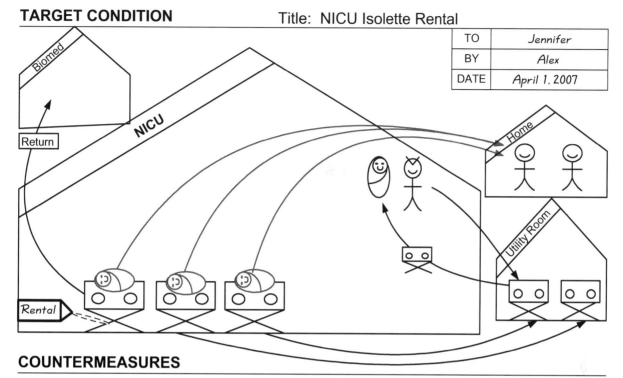

COUNTERMEASURES

1. Attach bright orange tags to rental isolettes when checked out of the Biomed department.
2. Print directions for returning the isolettes on the orange tag.
3. Half of the orange tag is retained in the Biomed department to track the rental equipment.

IMPLEMENTATION

What	Who	When	Outcome
Create rental return instructions	Biomed /RN	4/5/06	Instructions ready to print on tag
Create orange tags to be attached to rentals	Biomed /RN	4/10/06	Tags ready for use
Orient Biomed/NICU staff on new process	Biomed /NICU	4/15/06	New process implemented

COST/BENEFIT

Cost	$$$
Biomed and RN staff time	4 hours
Tag materials	$60
Benefit	$$$
Reduced rental fees ($63,000 - $27,800)	$35,200

TEST

Use tags for 6 weeks. Monitor weekly for possible revisions.

FOLLOW UP

October 22, 2007: Two tag revisions made in 6 weeks. In the 6 months after implementation, $27,800 spent on rental isolettes.

CASE STUDY 10: ICU SPINAL PRECAUTIONS

The issue for this A3 was raised by the family of a patient. While the family was at the bedside of their loved one, who had suffered a spinal injury in a fall, an aide coming on-shift in the afternoon was making her initial rounds, offering patients fresh water and other comfort measures. When she arrived in the room of the newly admitted patient, she offered to make him more comfortable by raising the head of his bed. The family, who had been advised by the physician that the patient must remain flat in bed until diagnostic films could confirm that it was safe to move him, were horrified that the hospital employee wanted to change his position. Fortunately, they advocated for the patient and no harm was done. When told of the directive, the patient care aide was mortified that her good intentions might have complicated the patient's injury.

The incident was then reviewed with the nursing and aide staff and more stories of similar incidents were confided. They agreed that the current system, in which the nurses and aides reported for duty at the same time, created a problem. Nurses routinely went into the report room to receive the handoff information from the day shift nurses, and the aides went directly on the floor to offer routine comfort measures to patients. After the unit report was received, the RN would review information pertinent to the patients being cared for by her team. Depending on the census and complexity of patient health issues, the report at the beginning of the shift would last from 30 to 45 minutes. An aide would be unaware of special needs of the patients until the nurse with whom she was teamed was out of the shift-to-shift nursing report.

The first suggestion was to include the aides in the unit report, which would have required an additional 30 to 45 minutes of shift time for the previous shift's aides. This seemed expensive and unpredictable. (What if the census was low and report was short?)

The next suggestion considered changing the shift times to stagger the arrival of the aides and nurses to allow the off-going aides who were familiar with the patients to continue care

On discussion with representatives of both nursing and the aide staff, no downside was recognized, and they agreed to use this schedule for a month. Follow-up survey and evaluation was scheduled for 2, 4, and 6 weeks after the initiation of the schedule. At those intervals, the response for continuing was positive.

In the staff review of this A3, the concern for *anyone* inadvertently changing the bed position was raised. It was agreed that a clear signal was needed at the patient's bedside that would alert the spinal precautions warning. A small, bright orange, inexpensive magnet was designed that could be placed adjacent to the bed-raising controls. In addition, a bright sign that defined spinal precautions was created; to be hung on the foot of the patient's bed, it could clearly be read by anyone entering the room.

MUDAs (sources of waste): Confusion, Defects

ROOT CAUSE:

- Aide on duty without specific patient safety information
- No clear signal that patient's bed shouldn't be adjusted

COUNTERMEASURES:

- Stagger aide/nurse shifts so that no aide is caring for patients without safety information
- Post clear definitions and warnings at the point of care

Relationship to the FOUR RULES IN USE:

- **Rule 1: Specify the work** (*Notice and details of spinal precautions not available to staff and families.*) See Figure 9-15.

ISSUE *Patient with unstable spinal fracture at risk of being moved inadvertantly.*

BACKGROUND

The neurologist was waiting to review patients X-ray before clearing him to be moved.
Shift-to-shift patient report takes approximately 45 minutes.

CURRENT CONDITION

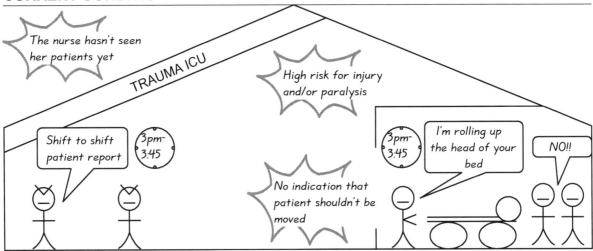

PROBLEM ANALYSIS

1. High risk of patient injury and/or paralysis
        Why? Aide not aware that patlent has unstable spinal fracture
            Why? Aide has not received patient report from nurse
                Why? Nurse is still receiving report from the nurse on the previous shift
                    Why? Nurse and aide begin their shift at the same time
      Why? No clear indication in room that patient shouldn't be moved
        Why? Spinal injury precautions aren't posted at point of care

Figure 9–15. A3 for ICU spinal precautions.

TARGET CONDITION

Title: ICU Spinal Precautions

TO	Dan
BY	Amy
DATE	November 15, 2006

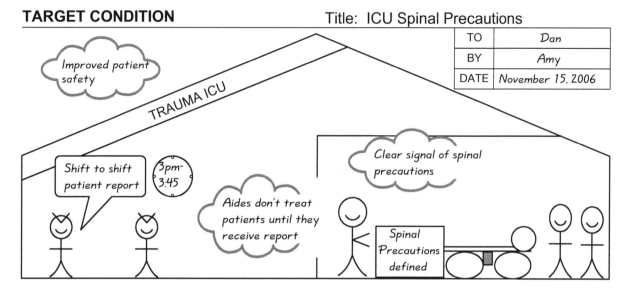

COUNTERMEASURES

1. Stagger aide and nurse shifts by 45 minutes.
2. Place "Spinal Precautions" magnet next to the patient's bed control.
3. Post a clear, visible magnet with list of spinal precautions on the foot of the patient's bed.

IMPLEMENTATION PLAN

What	Who	When	Outcome
Stagger aide shifts	Charge nurse	11/30/04	Aides receive report at the beginning of their shift
Create "Spinal Precautions" magnet	Dan	11/30/04	Place magnet next to the bed control of spinal precautions patients
Create magnet with spinal precautions list	Dan	12/05/04	Place magnet on the foot of the patient's bed
Orient staff at staff meeting	Charge nurse	12/10/04	Staff informed

COST/COST BENEFIT

Cost	$$$
Magnet/sign supplies	$104.00
Cost Benefit/waste recognition	$$$
Patient safety	Quality

TEST

Test effectiveness with paper signs taped to patient bed. Test results: Yes!

FOLLOW UP

January 15, 2007

Unit educator agreed to monitor use of magnet set for patients with spinal precautions.

2 weeks –   yes ☑   no ☐
4 weeks –   yes ☑   no ☐
6 weeks-   yes ☑   no ☐

CASE STUDY 11: EKG LEADS

An emergency nurse authored this A3 after an unpleasant experience with a physician. While the angry physician was legitimate in demanding improvement, the nurse chose to get to the *root cause* of the problem rather than hastening to a cumbersome, expensive, and demoralizing attempt to "train" the problem away. When a process is at fault, and can be corrected, the improvement is much more likely to succeed and be sustained than when workers rely on memory and training. This A3 demonstrates a wonderful example of that strategy.

The MD had ordered an urgent cardiogram (EKG) on a patient admitted to the ED with chest pain. Some confusing information on review of the EKG indicated that the leads had been inadvertently misapplied, and the test would have to be repeated. The machine was located quickly and the exam readministered.

After the patient was treated and the risk abated, the distressed physician addressed the charge nurse with the irate suggestion that the nurses be reeducated on proper lead placement to avoid this happening again.

The nurse, who had recently learned the A3 process, chose to investigate why this had occurred, rather than following his suggestion, which she was sure would be demeaning to the experienced nurses and expensive and difficult to arrange. She went to the nurse involved with the event, and together they examined the machine. Two significant things were noted.

First, the identifiers on some of the twelve leads were worn off from use. While the nurses did this procedure commonly, and there were several differently colored lead wires to help keep them straight, in times of high stress, with a critically injured patient, relying on memory sometimes failed.

The second thing noted was that the EKG cart did not contain an anatomical guideline to remind the operator of where to apply the leads. The nurses had been trained on such a tool and recalled seeing one at some previous time.

The charge nurse removed the leads that were missing labels from the machine and went to the Biomed department to exchange the leads. When the Biomed staff person saw the leads, he pulled new labels from a drawer at his desk and immediately fixed the unlabeled-lead problem. He also produced an anatomical reference card for the machine. It was then laminated and affixed to the cart for easy reference during the procedure.

To ensure that this event was not replayed, labels were included at the point of use—in the drawer of the cart—to be handy for replacement as the current ones wore. A sticker was placed on the top of the cart indicating their location in the drawer to support this becoming a customary practice.

This seems like a small effort, but consider the following points of value:

- Rapid diagnosis of emergency chest pain patients was more likely.

- Confusion was removed from a critical diagnostic process.

- Physician and RN confidence and relationships were improved.

- Nurse morale was preserved.

- Patient could be moved out of the ED more quickly and another patient could be seen sooner.

MUDAS (sources of waste): Confusion, Waiting, Overprocessing, Defects

Relationship to the 4 RULES IN USE:

- **Rule 1: Work not clearly specified.** (*There was no process for replacing defective labeling on the EKG machine.*)

- **Rule 4:** (*The initially suggested solution for improvement [re-training staff] did not get to the root of the problem and would not have assured that the problem wouldn't occur again.*) See Figure 9-16.

ISSUE   *Patient's diagnosis and care is delayed by inaccurate 12-lead electrocardiogram (EKG).*

BACKGROUND

November 1 - December 15: Three 12-lead EKGs repeated in ED due to incorrect placement of EKG leads. Average time of repeated EKG to MD = 31 minutes.

CURRENT CONDITION

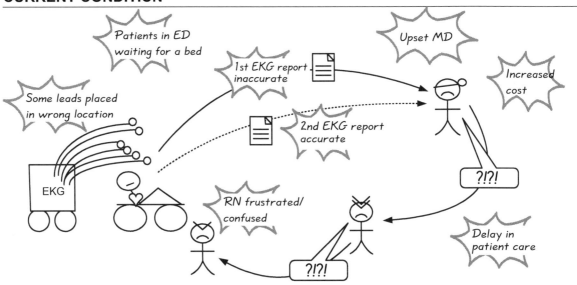

PROBLEM ANALYSIS

1. Delay in patient's treatment
        Why? EKG needs to be repeated
                Why? Some leads placed incorrectly on patient
                        Why? Leads aren't clearly identified (marks worn off)
2. Increased cost to hospital and patient
        Why? Redundant RN/MD work
        Why? Wasted materials/use of EKG machine
        Why? Other patients can't be seen
3. RN frustration and confusion
        Why? No clear signal for EKG lead placement
                Why? Leads aren't clearly identified (markers worn off)
        Why? MD is upset
                Why? Concern for patient/delay in diagnosis
                        Why? Incorrect EKG
                                Why? Leads aren't clearly marked
                Why? Bottleneck in flow of the ED patients
                        Why? Bed occupied by patient awaiting cardiac diagnosis
                                Why? EKG needs to be repeated (as above)
                Why? His time is misused trying to get correct EKG

Figure 9–16. A3 for EKG leads.

TARGET CONDITION

Title: EKG Leads

TO	John
BY	Lynn
DATE	January 1, 2007

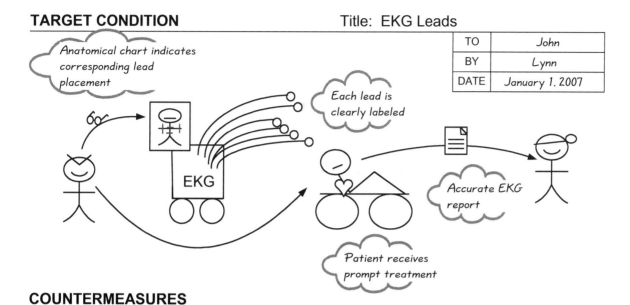

Anatomical chart indicates corresponding lead placement

Each lead is clearly labeled

Accurate EKG report

Patient receives prompt treatment

EKG

COUNTERMEASURES

1. Clearly label EKG leads
2. Create system for replacing labels when worn.
3. Create anatomical chart for lead placement on EKG cart

IMPLEMENTATION PLAN

What	Who	When	Outcome
Label EKG leads	Biomed	2/1/06	Clear signal to RN for lead placement
System for lead label replacement	Biomed	2/2/06	Clear process for replacement of labels
Inservice for staff	RN	2/4/06	Staff aware of replacement process
Laminate and adhere anatomical chart to EKG cart	RN	2/4/06	Staff aware of process

COST/BENEFIT

Cost	$$$
Labels (12 x $0.50 x 2 EKG machines)	$12.00
Benefit	$$$
Increase capacity in Emergency Department	Quality and $$$
Patient receives prompt treatment	Quality

TEST

RN does EKG on simulated patient w/anatomical chart and marked leads – completed in 9 minutes.

FOLLOW UP

February 15, 2007 – May 15, 2007:
No repeated EKGs.
Average time of EKG to MD – 11 minutes.

Appendices

A. 7 Mudas of Healthcare

B. Guidelines for Making an Observation of Work in Progress

C. Observation Worksheet

D. Legend of Drawing Symbols

E. A3 Quick Reference

F. A3 Review Guidelines

G. Meeting Evaluation Form

H. Guidelines for Conducting a Lean Meeting

I. Resources on the WWW

APPENDIX A: 7 MUDAS OF HEALTHCARE

Taiichi Ohno, credited with creating the Toyota Production System in the 1950s, defined for manufacturing seven types of waste that describe all activity that adds cost but not value.

WASTE "MUDA"	Definition	Examples
Confusion	People doing the work are not confident about the best way to perform tasks	Same activities being performed in different ways by different people Unclear MD orders Unclear route for medicine administration Unclear system for indicating charges for billing
Motion	Movement of people that does not add value	Looking for information Looking for materials and people Materials, tools located far from the work
Waiting	Idle time created when people, information, equipment, or materials are not at hand	Waiting for other workers at meetings, surgeries, procedures, reports Patients waiting for appointments, MD visits, procedures
Processing	Activities that do not add value from the patient/customers perspective	Clarifying orders Redundant information gathering/charting Missing medications Regulatory paperwork
Inventory	More materials on hand than are required to do the work	Overstocked medications on units Overstocked supplies on units and in warehouses
Defects	Work that contains errors or lacks something of value	Medication errors Rework Variation in outcomes Incorrect charges/billing Surgical errors
Over-production	Redundant work	Duplicate charting Multiple forms with same information Copies of reports sent automatically

Six of those seven are applicable to healthcare and are included with one addition below.
Recognizing waste in our organizations is the first and most essential step in transforming waste to wisdom.

Causes	Countermeasures
Lack of standardized specification of activities of work Lack of common language Workers relying on memory or "figuring things out"	All activities of work clearly specified Clear signals that trigger activities of work uniformly
Inconsistent information systems (includes communication) Materials stocking that does not match the demand Scheduling that creates "workarounds" and "rework"	IT systems that match the demand of work Reliable communication systems Fluid materials availability that meet the current demand Consistent scheduling that meets the demand
Poor understanding of the time required to do a task Poor accountability for delivering on time Compounding delays Unresponsiveness of scheduling systems to demand of work	"Right now" scheduling Fewer meetings; work done in small focus groups Matching capabilities to demand for services, supplies
Work area layout that does not promote continuous flow Complex flow of medication delivery from pharmacy Multiple/complex forms	Work area redesigns to create continuous flow Simplified/consistent delivery systems for meds/materials/information Forms that document only essential information
Supply/demand not well understood Outdated supplies not deleted Personal preferences catered, duplicated	Supply exactly what is needed; no more, no less Keep supply availability current Understand personal preferences and orchestrate "like" items use
Lack of understanding of what is "defect free" Lack of specification in work processes	System redesigns that support workers in doing their good work by clear specification of activities of work, clear expectations of outcomes and safe environment for problem solving in the course of work Clear definition/understanding of what is "defect free" Single, clearly understood method of addressing "defect free" right now
Misinterpretation of regulations Poor communication between departments, offices No clear specification of who needs what Computer systems not linked	Clear interpretation of regulations System (electronic or paper) of information traveling with patient that eliminates redundancy

APPENDIX B: GUIDELINES FOR MAKING AN OBSERVATION OF WORK IN PROGRESS.

Appendix C contains a sample observation sheet borrowed from manufacturing. Forms help to organize observations and analyze them when complete. Thorough note-taking can also assist in learning.

1. Choose an activity to observe (look at a process here, not the performance of an individual). While learning, choose a process that's easy to define with easily recognizable steps. Allow enough time to make a meaningful observation of the work as it happens; in short activities like "registering a patient for outpatient surgery," if you watch for 60 to 90 minutes, a number of the activities may be completed in the observed time that will offer more insight about the consistency of the process. When choosing something with many steps that occur over a protracted period of time, you will likely become less familiar and have less understanding of the process. Be easy on yourself as you're learning! The value of observation will become apparent quickly and your investigation skills will improve with practice.

2. Arrange for a convenient time to observe when there is plenty of activity. Introduce yourself to the staff doing the work and explain that you are observing the process and not the person. Be sure to engage workers in your observation. Let them know that you are making these observations and notes to recognize when and where their valuable time is being wasted. Encourage them to participate! You might miss subtle moves and nuances in the work, so ask them to point out workarounds and rework as they occur. Assure them that you will show them the results of your observation to validate it for accuracy.

3. Use the Observation Worksheet to document your observations; this will record what you see and help you sort the information after the event. There is so much to be learned from observation, and the goal is to identify spe-

cific problems to which you can apply the A3 problem-solving process.

- Fill out the worksheet demographic information completely.

- The blank box in the right upper corner of the sheet leaves room for the physical layout of the work area and perhaps a spaghetti diagram of the movement of people or products in the area.

- Decide on your time measurement. Generally, a 60 to 90 minute observation of work adequately measures the activities, but in an activity like lab specimen processing or prescription preparation, it may be more appropriate to measure in seconds. Whatever the case, stick to the same unit of measure throughout one observation session for consistency.

- When you begin to observe, disregard the icon columns in the center of the page and concentrate on what you see. Make a time entry whenever the worker changes activities. (For example, "10:01 filling prescription bottle" may be your first entry and at 10:02 the telephone rings; your second entry would be "10:02 answer telephone." If the person spent 2 minutes on the phone, then went back to filling the prescription bottle, the third entry would be "10:04 filling prescription bottle.")

Observe as long as it takes, to see at least one full activity completed, ideally observing more than one, for 60 to 90 minutes. Don't wear out your welcome and don't bore yourself to death! Simply take advantage of the many opportunities to observe and you will gain a good deal of information in relatively short time.

APPENDIX C: OBSERVATION WORKSHEET

OBSERVATION RECORD

ACTIVITY:

PERSON OBSERVED:

LOCATION:

DATE: OBSERVER:

LAYOUT OF WORK AREA

TIME	ACTIVITY	Operation	Transportation	Inspection	Clarification	Delay	Interruption	Locating	NOTES
: :		◯	⇨	∞	?	▽	⟁	⚡	
: :		◯	⇨	∞	?	▽	⟁	⚡	
: :		◯	⇨	∞	?	▽	⟁	⚡	
: :		◯	⇨	∞	?	▽	⟁	⚡	
: :		◯	⇨	∞	?	▽	⟁	⚡	
: :		◯	⇨	∞	?	▽	⟁	⚡	
: :		◯	⇨	∞	?	▽	⟁	⚡	
: :		◯	⇨	∞	?	▽	⟁	⚡	
: :		◯	⇨	∞	?	▽	⟁	⚡	
: :		◯	⇨	∞	?	▽	⟁	⚡	
: :		◯	⇨	∞	?	▽	⟁	⚡	
: :		◯	⇨	∞	?	▽	⟁	⚡	
: :		◯	⇨	∞	?	▽	⟁	⚡	
: :		◯	⇨	∞	?	▽	⟁	⚡	
: :		◯	⇨	∞	?	▽	⟁	⚡	
: :		◯	⇨	∞	?	▽	⟁	⚡	
: :		◯	⇨	∞	?	▽	⟁	⚡	
: :		◯	⇨	∞	?	▽	⟁	⚡	
: :		◯	⇨	∞	?	▽	⟁	⚡	
: :		◯	⇨	∞	?	▽	⟁	⚡	
: :		◯	⇨	∞	?	▽	⟁	⚡	
: :		◯	⇨	∞	?	▽	⟁	⚡	
: :		◯	⇨	∞	?	▽	⟁	⚡	
: :		◯	⇨	∞	?	▽	⟁	⚡	

APPENDIX D: LEGEND OF DRAWING SYMBOLS

Below are some symbol examples; as you create your own, include a simple legend on your A3 if necessary.

APPENDIX E: A3 QUICK REFERENCE

ISSUE

-What is the issue through the eyes of the customer/patient?

BACKGROUND

-Include information for understanding the issue.
  -when/where/how does it occur?
-Add data to objectively measure the issue.
-Include history that is pertinent to the issue.

CURRENT CONDITION

-Draw a diagram of how the work happens now.
-Highlight the problems with storm clouds.
-What about the problem is not defect-free?
- Can you measure the waste?

PROBLEM ANALYSIS

-List problems identified in the Current Condition (storm clouds).
-Ask WHY? five times to get to the root cause of the problem.

TARGET CONDITION   Title

	TO
	BY
	DATE

-Draw a diagram of a better way to do the work.
-Highlight the good features as fluffy clouds.
-Create measurable targets for the new way to work (quantity/time).

COUNTERMEASURES

-What are we going to do to get to the Target Condition?

IMPLEMENTATION PLAN

-How are we going to get there?

What	Who	When	Outcome

COST/BENEFIT

Cost	$$$
Expenses necessary for implementation	
Benefit	$$$
Dollar amount saved with implementation	
Quality gained with implementation	

TEST

-Can you design an experiment to test your implementation plan?

FOLLOW UP

-When was the follow-up was done?
-What are the actual result compared to the anticipated results?
-The follow-up becomes the new current condition for continued improvement.

APPENDIX F: A3 REVIEW GUIDELINES[1]

By Durward Sobek
Cindy Jimmerson

This document provides a small list of questions, section by section, for the reviewer to ask when reading an A3 problem-solving report.

Issue:

- Does the issue give a good description of what the report is about?
- Is it too long or too short?

Background:

- Is the context clear enough to understand how the issue fits within the larger organization and goals?
- Do you understand the history of the problem?
- Do you understand why the problem is important to the patient, worker, or organization?

Current Condition:

- Can you easily and quickly grasp how the current process works?
- Are the specific problems identified with storm clouds?
- Has the problem(s) been quantified?
- Was the information gathered from actual observation or direct interview with the subject of the problem?

Cause Analysis

- Has the author identified the most important problems to address for this issue?
- Do the problems addressed correspond to a storm cloud in the previous section?

---

1. National Science Foundation Grant No. 0115352.

- Has the analysis gone to enough depth? Are the root(s) of the problem(s) clearly and sufficiently identified?
- Have the problems been defined as: a) failure to specify an **activity**, b) ambiguous, complex, or nonexistent **connections**, and/or c) complex **pathways**?

To and By Lines:

- Is the recipient identified?
- Is the author identified?
- Is it dated?

Target Condition

- Can you easily and quickly grasp how the new process will work?
- Have countermeasures[1] been identified with fluffy clouds?
- Does the set of countermeasures address the complete set of problems identified in the cause analysis?
- Does the proposed target condition move the organization closer to Ideal? (what the patient needs—defect free, immediate, on demand, one-at-a-time, without waste, safe for all.)

Implementation Plan

- Does the plan cover the set of countermeasures identified in the target condition?
- Has each activity in the plan been specified as to who, what, and when? (i.e., content, sequence, timing, and outcome)
- Is the plan doable?

Follow-Up

- Does the follow-up plan predict *measurable* results?

---

1. A countermeasure is a specific change to the process that will address a problem and move the process closer to Ideal. In other words, the specific changes that make the target different from the current condition.

- Do you know when the follow-up test will occur and who will do it?
- Are all problems not addressed with countermeasures identified, with plans to study later?
- Has space been reserved to report actual results?

Overall Questions

- Have all the people affected by the proposed changes been consulted? Do they all agree to the changes?
- Has the author reached enough specificity?
- Does the story flow well? Is the report neat and organized? Is it easy to read?
- Is it clear who will approve the implementation plan?
- Is the report complete enough to satisfy an external reviewer?

APPENDIX G: MEETING EVALUATION FORM

MEETING EVALUATION FORM

Name/Purpose of Meeting: _____

Time planned for meeting _____ Actual time in meeting _____

Participants: Clerical _____ RN _____ Manager _____ TechnicianMD _____

Administrator _____ Other _____

Number of minutes relevant to me/my work: (Tic marks →) _____

From the current agenda, could you create an ACTIVITY DESIGN?

Activity   **Time * * 15 * * 30 * * 45 * * 60 * * 75 * * 90 * * 105 * * 120**

1. _____
2. _____
3. _____
4. _____
5. _____
6. _____

Could you create an implementation plan from the meeting discussion?

What	Who	When	Outcome

Reflection:

How much of the meeting was value-added to my work? (review tic marks) _____

_____

What was the labor cost of the meeting? _____

Did the value of the meeting justify the cost?_____ My participation? _____

_____

Was the agenda realistic?_____ Was the time allowed adequate? _____

Did the participants leave understanding the implementation plan? _____

_____

Could the work have been done better by a small focus group (2–3 people)_____

APPENDIX H: GUIDELINES FOR CONDUCTING A LEAN MEETING USING THE A3 PROCESS

Ahead of time: Prepare the members (as few as possible to represent the parties involved with the issue to the fact that they will be using a new approach and focus primarily on one topic; be sure there is a whiteboard or flipchart and pens for drawing.

Using principles of A3 Problem Solving, a meeting leader would conduct a meeting with the following format:

1. Identify a meeting leader (who understands the A3 process).
2. Introduce members (representing the parties affected by the process/problem).
3. Define the process of a lean meeting and proceed.
    - Define a single issue on which to focus.
    - Assign responsibility of drawing on the board to one member.
    - Have one member draw a paper copy as you progress.

The lean meeting leader (with the group) will:

1. Establish how the work happens now (have assigned person draw on the whiteboard).
2. Determine the problems (go around the table and have each of the affected parties include their concerns) and add where these problems occur on the drawing as storm clouds.
3. Analyze those problems to determine the root cause.
    a. Ask five whys.
4. Determine and draw a target condition on which each affected party agrees.
5. Agree on countermeasures.
6. Create a realistic implementation plan to assign accountability for tasks.
    a. What's going to happen?
    b. Who will do it?
    c. When will it be complete?
    d. What's the expected outcome of each task?
7. Establish date/time/place to reconvene and report results of implementation plan.
8. Design a test of the plan.
9. Get approval of implementation plan and test.
10. Use current condition, target condition, implementation plan, and test as minutes of meeting and distribute.
11. Conduct test.
12. Meet again; report results to group and accept or redesign.
13. If satisfied . . . IMPLEMENT!
14. Schedule and conduct follow-up review.

APPENDIX I: RESOURCES

INTERNET

1. Author's participation in original research funded by a National Science Foundation Grant: www.coe.montana.edu/ie/faculty/sobek/ioc_grant/IERC_2004.pdf.

2. Reading about A3 problem solving: http://archives.fandm mag.com/publication/article.jsp?pubId=1&id=34 http://www.sme.org/cgi-bin/get-newsletter.pl?LEAN&20060309&2&.

3. General information about A3s and lean courses:

   www.leanhealthcarewest.com
   www.leanhealthcareperformance.com
   www.onesourcetrainingiowa.com (Iowa)
   www.scmep.org (South Carolina)
   www.leaninnovationsinc.com (Canada)
   www.leanhealthcareeurope.com (Denmark)
   www.cmtc.com (California)
   www.vmec.org (Vermont)

4. A3 archiving/sharing: www.improvementmarquee.com.

5. Effective Coaching: http://www.1000ventures.com/business_guide/crosscuttings/coaching_main.html

   www.dau.mil/pubs/arq/2004arq/Brown.pdf.

6. eVSM/eA3 software: www.evsm.com.

BOOKS

1. Jimmerson, Cindy. *reVIEW™ Workbook: Realizing Exceptional Value in Everyday Work*. Missoula, MT., 2007.

2. Rother, Mike and John Shook. *Learning to See: Value Stream Mapping to Add Value and Eliminate Muda*. Cambridge, MA, LEI, 1999.

3. Tapping, Don, et. al. *Value Stream Management: Eight Steps to Planning, Mapping and Sustaining Lean Improvements*. New York, Productivity Press, 2002.

Glossary of Terms

A3: The name "A3" refers to the European/Asian name of 11″ × 17″ paper, on which an A3 report is drawn. A3 problem s)olving is documented on this size paper.

A3 Document: Parts include: The Issue, Background/ Measurement, Current Condition, Problem Analysis, Target Condition, Countermeasures, Implementation Plan, Cost and Cost Benefit/Waste Recognition, The Test, Follow-Up.

Changeover Time (C/O): Time required to prepare staff and environment for the next patient.

Clear Signal: Easy-to-interpret visual or auditory cue for next activity that prevents confusion or error and promotes continuous flow.

"Command And Control" Management: A business model that does not encourage *deep thinking* at all levels; rather, problems are reported and decisions made up the ladder, thus locking out the collective intelligence of the organization.

Continuous Flow: Work that proceeds without interruption or waste.

Countermeasures: Changes that must be implemented in the A3 process to move from the current to the target condition.

Current Condition: A simple sketch of the observed way that the issue occurred.

Defect Free: Exactly what the patient needs, i.e., services received without defect.

eVSM/eA3: A simple "drop & drag" software that supports lean practitioners in drawing, sharing, and analyzing value stream maps and A3 reports.

Five Whys: The concept of asking a series of causal questions in order to discover the root cause of a problem.

The 4 Rules in Use: Activities, Connections, Pathway, Improvement.

Ideal: Defect Free, One by One, On Demand, Immediate Response to Problems.

Lean: Refers to those operational strategies derived from the Toyota Production System.

Muda: Japanese word for "waste."

The 7 Mudas for Healthcare (seven sources of waste): Confusion, Motion, Waiting, Processing, Inventory, Defects, Overproduction.

Non-Value Added Time: Time where the patient or product sits with nothing happening.

Pathway: Steps in the delivery of a service or product.

Storm Clouds: Problems associated with the current condition.

Takt Time: The calculated time that you should produce to meet the demand.

An example of calculating Takt:

- If the average patient in an urgent care center demands 30 minutes of care, the Takt would be calculated like this:

- 1,260 (number of minutes in a 8 hour shift) divided by 30 minutes (time needed per patient) multiplied by 3 (nurses available in that 8 hours) = 42 patients that could be cared for in an 8-hour shift by 3 nurses.

Target Condition: The proposed better way to work.

Toyota Production System (TPS): Toyota Motor Company's industry-leading business model.

Value-Added Time: Time where the patient actually sees value, or when activities are essential to the process.

Value Stream Map: A time-and-motion graphic representation of work that illustrates value and non-value-added activities that occur when requesting and fulfilling an order for a product or service.

Waste: Any activities that do not add value to the patient or customer.

Index

C

D

E

About the Author

CINDY JIMMERSON, President, Lean Healthcare West

Ms. Jimmerson is a pioneer of lean healthcare, with an extensize background in emergency systems development and healthcare education. She initiated her work with a grant from the National Science Foundation, 2001–2004. She is the founder and president of Lean Healthcare West, an organization of healthcare professionals offering education and implementation of TPS/Lean principles in hospital, clinic, and long-term care facilities. She is the author of the reVIEW® Course and Workbook and many journal publications. Although she travels internationally for work, she refuses to budge her office from the beautiful Blackfoot River in Missoula, Montana.

ABOUT HEALTHCARE PERFORMANCE PRESS

At Healthcare Performance Press, a division of Productivity Press, our mission is to be the primary source of leading-edge publications, workbooks, tools, and resources that support and educate healthcare professionals and other stakeholders in the drive to improve the overall performance and quality of the healthcare system.

Our publications are written by industry thought leaders who offer proven, practical, and thought-provoking information and strategies in subjects ranging from lean methodologies to financial management, strategy and leadership, information technology and patient safety and quality.

For more information on current and forthcoming publications and for additional resources, please visit our website at HCPpress.com

+Healthcare
Performance Press
A Division of Productivity Press